GIRL TO WOMAN

OTHER BOOKS BY SUSAN HAUSER

Meant To Be Read Out Loud

Which Way to Look

What the Animals Know

Redpoll on a Broken Branch

GIRL TO
WOMAN
a gathering of images

Susan Hauser

Portland   Maine

Astarte Shell Press
P.O. Box 10453
Portland, Maine 04104

Library of Congress Cataloging-in-Publication Data

Hauser, Susan, 1942-
    Girl to woman: a gathering of images/by Susan Hauser
        p. cm.
    ISBN 0-9624626-4-0 (pbk.): $10.95
    1. Hauser, Susan, 1942- -Biography. 2. Authors, American-20th century-Biography
    3. Women-United States-Social life and customs   I. Title
    PS3558.A7588Z466   1992
    818.5409-dc20   92-31603
    [B]   CIP

Book Design, Cover & Illustrations by Sylvia Sims, Portland
Typesetting by L&L Kern, Portland
Printed in the USA by McNaughton & Gunn, Saline, Michigan

1st Printing, 1992

10   9   8   7   6   5   4   3   2   1

ACKNOWLEDGEMENTS

Some of these essays and poems first appeared in the following publications: *Border Crossings* anthology, *Caprice* magazine, *Lake Street Review* magazine, *Loonfeather* anthology, *Loonfeather* magazine, *Mpls St Paul* magazine, *Poets Who Haven't Moved to Minneapolis* anthology, *Sing Heavenly Muse!* journal, *Woman Poet: The Midwest,* anthology. Some of the essays have been aired on KAXE Community Radio, Grand Rapids, Minnesota.

CONTENTS

STILL, FOREVER
A Personal Girlhood

c. 1952

Part One

Part Two

Epilogue

Part One

UNDER
THE EAVES

      I AM five or six years old. Or eight or nine. I wish I could remember. I am sitting cross legged in the middle of the living room floor. The carpet is rose beige, with maroon roses looped and linked across its fibers. Rose beige drapes hang in waiting at the sides of the triple window. The room is light, although there is no sunlight on the floor.

      I think the television is on, but I'm not sure. I think I am alone in the room, but I am not sure of that either. A brand new never before felt feeling moves through my body, starting down at the bottom somewhere and flowing up through me the way sunlight breaks through clouds sometimes, briefly, and illuminating all that it touches.

      Then it is gone. I go to my mother. "Something funny has happened," I tell her.

"What?"

"I don't know. Just something funny I felt. It's gone now."

"Well, then it's okay."

      I return to the living room, hesitate, then sit again in the spot where I had been sitting. Nothing happens.

THAT WAS in the Richfield house. We lived there until the summer I was twelve. Most of my memories from there are like the one of that first orgasm: bubbles of consciousness in a world that had no horizons, no perspective. Each incident is its own fact, and nothing more. Even the people, my mother included, are mere presences in these memories. Ghosts of themselves. I cannot see their faces, or their clothes. I don't remember what room my mother was in when I went to talk to her, though I do think she was folding clothes, or putting them away. She was larger, taller than I was, and carried out her tasks in a world clearly on a different plane, one above my straight line of sight, and indistinct. It had nothing to do with me.

The house itself I do remember. All of it was mine. I was a snooper. I knew what was in every closet, even the ones I wasn't supposed to go into. I even knew what was behind the panel in my upstairs closet. The plywood sheet was held in place by four wing nuts. They were easy to turn and the panel was easy to pry loose, but it was not easy to drag out of the way of the opening, since I had to close the closet door, to conceal my illegitimate activity, and had about three square feet of working space.

The closet bulb was puny and cast inadequate light on the mysteries under the eaves. The sharply slanted and rough wood of the roof boards caught at my hair as I leaned in to try to look all the way down to the ends of the house, first one way, then the other. Past the second or third roof supports, the space fell into utter darkness.

Pulling back, I kneeled to inspect the pink cotton candy stuff on the floor. I pressed one hand down into it. It seemed to have no bottom, although I knew the living room ceiling was down there somewhere. But how far? It was like the street-spanning spring puddles I was afraid to bicycle through. Clouds tore across their surfaces, and I was more than half convinced that at least one of those puddles was as deep as the sky and I would disappear into it forever and the water would close over me and the clouds would skate across the surface and not tell where I was.

Still on my knees, I peered again into the long dark to my right and my left. How could I get down there? I discovered the stringers under the cotton candy, but what if they did not go all the way to the ends? And what if my knees slipped off them and I fell into that infinite pink, or slipped right through it into the living room itself?

I did not ease my small body into the cave of the eaves. I did go into the closet sometimes, though, and peer down into the twin tunnels. And one spring, I did ride right through the middle of the puddle that commanded all four corners of 74th Street and Emerson Avenue. Pulse racing, feet pounding on the pedals, I aimed for the center of the puddle. The streets were dirt, and as my bike sank into the soft center ground, my legs froze and I closed my eyes and the black water of fear closed over me. When I looked again, my legs were pumping me down the dry middle of the road faster than clouds are carried by a March wind.

BABY
DOLL

MY FIRST memory is a crib memory. The crib is in the big bedroom in the Richfield house, on the south wall, just inside the door and to the left as you enter. The other kids' beds are on the other side of the room. I know they are there, but in my picture, they are blurred, the way things are in a dream sometimes, the only clear space being the very immediate surroundings.

My Aunt Marcia is bent over the crib, leaning down at me from the blur. Uncle Joe is sitting in the living room on the love seat that is on the south wall, where the piano would be later.

That's all. Last year I told my Uncle Joe about this. He was astonished. "We were baby sitting. You started to cry. Your mother told Marcia if you were unhappy to give you a hanky. You would rub it between your fingers and would stop crying. Marcia went into the bedroom and you became quiet. When she came out I asked what she had done, and she said 'I used a hanky.' I didn't know about your habit, and I thought she had stuffed a hanky in your mouth—I leaped up and ran into the bedroom. The crib was on the south wall, just inside the door."

9

I don't remember Marcia giving me the hanky, just her leaning over the crib, close down to me, enveloping me. And how could I know about the sofa in the living room, and where Joe was sitting? How did I know it was Marcia and Joe, and not some other grownups? Did I really remember the event, or was it a family joke, told over and over, about how Marcia "shut me up with a hanky?" Hearing it, did I recall the bedroom, familiar to my older eye, and place myself in the crib, and draw Marcia leaning over me? Were there pictures or movies of the living room, one with Uncle Joe sitting on the love seat?

Or do I remember?

THE BEDROOM comes into focus again. This time my bed is on the east wall, also just inside the door, but to the right. I am older — in grade school? I have a recurrent pervasive pain the length of my right thigh. It is deep inside, wedged between muscle and bone. Rubbing does not reach it. Mother cannot help. "Growing pains," she says. "It will go away."

Forty years later, I still have it. When it comes on, I lie flat on my back and bring my knee up to my chest. By adjusting the angle of bone to breast, I can locate the strand of pain. One hand on my shin bone, one on my knee, I tighten the Z of lower leg, upper leg and torso. The muscle yields. I let my breath out, relax my spine. Tighten the Z again, slowly. Then again. Then slowly release it. The muscle sighs as it settles down in its fleshy cradle, and I sleep.

I remember Mother leaning over my bed, trying to comfort me. I remember my anger and fear that she could not. How could there be nothing she could do? Didn't she care? Was she lying? Or was their pain for which there is no solace? I pulled my disdain inside myself and clung to it.

MY HANKY habit became known in the family as "hankying." I was the only one who did it. I still do it. All I need is some good cotton cloth — a tee-shirt, a bathrobe. Sheeting. I have stopped sucking my tongue up into the roof hollow of my mouth.

I hankied with intent. I held one of Mother's linen hankies, probably smelling good, between the thumb and index finger of my left hand (this I just discover now, as I try it with my right — I am definitely a left-handed hankier). I doubled the fabric over, and as I moved my index finger back and forth along the inside of my thumb, the two surfaces glided back and forth on each other. Simultaneously, I sucked on my tongue, making a little squooshy noise I could hear in my head.

One day when I was in seventh grade a friend and I were walking to school. I guess I was hankying. She said I would have to stop that someday. That had never occurred to me — no one had mentioned it before. I tried to give it up and realized it would be hard to do. I would work at it in stages. First I would quit sucking my tongue, and that I did.

Soon after, I gave up my baby doll. We had moved to the house at Spring Lake. I decided I had to put her away. I took her down to the basement, rocked her, talked to her, and laid her to rest in a box and put her in a closet. Years later, when my husband and I were moving one more time and cleaning things out, she surfaced again and I stuffed her in a plastic trash bag and sent her away for good. It was the right thing to do, at the time.

MY BABY doll must have had a name. I don't remember it. I remember her. She had a soft, stuffed torso and a wooden head, with little curls carved onto it and painted brown, and eyes that opened and closed with a clicking sound, and a perfect nose and a little red mouth. Her rubber legs were stitched to her torso but her rubber arms were snapped into sockets set inside her chest. I could turn them up and down and even all the way around. They were held in place by a rubber band attached to hooks on the socket end of each arm. This I found out when the band broke. Who fixed it, using a crochet hook to slip the rubber sinew into place? And how did her head come off that time? Mother and I took her to the doll hospital. I didn't want to leave her there, but the woman talked me into it.

My baby doll could cry. Not wet tears, like they do now, but an audible cry. I turned her on her belly and then to her back and she whimpered and I consoled her. I never wondered what made her cry until Brooks wanted to know. We cut her chest open so we could see. We found a little round box right where her heart would be, if baby dolls had hearts. Mother must have sewed her up for me, but somehow the box got broken and I would turn her onto her belly, and then up, and her eyes would click and she would stare at me in silence. This I was learning to understand as well: sometimes it is best to keep your own counsel.

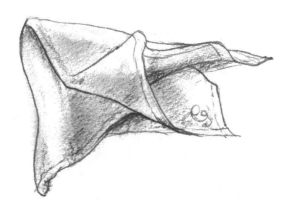

THE RICHFIELD HOUSE

c.1945

WHEN I think of the Richfield house now, I see it from kitty corner across 73rd Street. I don't think I ever stood there and looked at the house that way, but that is the angle of the only full-face photograph I have. The image is mostly right for me: a white frame house, mature oak trees in the front yard. Not planted yet are the three pine trees that commanded the side yard the last time I drove by there, each with an eight foot diameter skirt and tops I could have peered into from my upstairs bedroom window and that, when younger and smaller, were refuge in hide-and-seek. The street is not paved. There is no upstairs. Was I born yet?

The house is on the corner of 73rd and Emerson. 1201 West 73rd Street. The front half of the lot slopes down to 73rd and is dug out in front of the basement, where the garage is. Steps lead up to the front door. The back door, off the kitchen, opens onto the level back yard.

The Richfield house. It was not a tag for me when I lived there, the way it is now, a way of locking certain memories into the calendar: "That was in Richfield." And I didn't experience it as temporary, as the first house in a sequence of houses, the way it sounds when I talk about it now.

I also did not think of it as permanent, because I did not think about the future. I did not even think about bedtime until I was tired, or meals until I was hungry. What a little animal I was, nose to the ground, looking up only when something too tall or slippery got in my way.

The house was my burrow. In our upstairs bedroom, Cary Lou — Karen Louise — and I rummaged by day, and at night curled up together in a tangle of arms and legs. I was not aware of this until the night I awoke to a flashlight beam, covers pulled back and my parents and some other grownups giggling over us. In her nightly cruise of the upstairs rooms, pulling blankets back over our still bodies, Mother had discovered our entanglement.

THERE WERE two bedrooms upstairs, Cary Lou's and mine at the west end, Brooks and Nicky's at the east. There was a long hall between the two, with the closets that reached in under the eaves, and a bathroom at one end of the stairway that ran parallel to the hall. The stairwell was open, guarded by a railing.

The walls were knotty pine. In the mornings I stared at the dark, red blood of the knots as it seeped into the grain of the wood, and discovered faces and animals and flowers and bursts of beings that I could not prove lived anywhere on earth. Some of them I was afraid of and had to look at even longer to turn them into something else, so they would not watch me while I slept.

I remember when the upstairs was added. Papa Jack, my Dad's father, was a contractor and he came and worked there with some other men and I loved being near him all day, and I loved running my hand on the sanded-to-silk rail that led up the stairs and saying over and over "This is the house that Jack built, this is the house that Jack built." I felt very brave to be calling him Jack, and he would reach out and catch at me as I sneaked past him. It was an extension of the morning game we played when I stayed over night with him and Ma. They had twin beds, and when I woke up I would leave the back bedroom and climb in with Ma, and Papa Jack and I would stretch our arms into the gap between the beds and take turns slapping at each other's palms, trying to get our hands away before they could be caught.

I must have been seven or eight or nine when we moved upstairs, because Nicky must have been old enough to sleep there — three or four? — and I am four years older. Before that all five of us slept in the big bedroom downstairs. Gretchen was nearly nine when Nicky was born. Nine years of babies nested in one room, dreaming to each other's breathing. Mom and Dad got the big room next. Gretchen got her own bedroom, theirs, around the corner of the little hall that also linked one end of the living room to the kitchen.

THE KITCHEN was huge, though it had not always been. Before the upstairs was added it had been more than doubled in space. The new part was not a dinette, not a dining room, not a family room, not an entryway. It was all of those. It was where we sat on the floor and pulled on our leggings and boots in the mornings, and where we sat again, in puddles of dirt and water, and pulled them off in the afternoon. It was where all seven of us ate dinner, at a rectangular yellow table that had a little, tiny metal ledge turned up underneath it, where Nicky stored green beans.

It was where Mother opened her sewing machine sometimes and let me make doll clothes, and where she sat at a small desk and did things I didn't understand.

In the old part of the kitchen, the sink was laid into the southeast corner of the cupboard, and windows looked both ways so you could see almost all of Emerson Avenue as it dropped down the hill to 73rd on the left, and to the right pulled away into that scary part of the neighborhood where you didn't know every kid's name. And you could see straight across the street to the vacant lot where the boys had a fort.

EMERSON AVENUE was our playground. We stayed off 73rd, except to cross it over to Kimm's, and except for the time we had great big cardboard boxes and put them in the middle of the road and took turns sitting in them, the tops pulled closed, waiting for cars to go by.

On Emerson, bikes and kids flew in and out of driveways and yards the way birds fly in a forest. The dirt of the center of the road was especially good for marbles, giving way to our spoons and accommodating our elbows and knees. And in the spring the soft soil of the cut bank in front of St. Martin's yielded up baby toads by the handful. We dug into the earth, making houses and fences and naming the little beasts and trying to make them stay in their yards. The bank crawled with them, and with us.

The milkman came on Emerson Avenue, in the summer parking his truck in the shade of a tree, water leaking out the back as ice yielded to the heat. Sometimes he would give us crystalline chunks to suck on, treasures too slippery to hold onto for long.

One time in the winter Mom let me leave a bottle of milk outside to freeze so I could see how ice is bigger than water. The frozen cream rose out of the collar of glass, a headless neck rising out of a body.

WOOD LAKE

IT IS a bright October day. Karen and I pull on our sweaters and go out to walk. Bill and I have just moved to Mud Lake, and I want to show her the swamp. We inch down the steep hill, holding onto shrubs and deadfall, our shoes slipping on the dried leaves.

At the bottom of the hill we stand facing a wall of swamp grass, taller than a child and almost as tall as we are. The yellowing reeds click in the wind coming off the bay.

"Doesn't it remind you of Wood Lake?"

"It *is* Wood Lake."

We start walking again, pulled along by the narrow string of the animal path that stitches the hill to the swamp. When we come to a wider, human path, we turn onto it and pick our way out into the swamp to the grassy island that is a good stone's throw from shore. We climb to its crest and let ourselves down into deer beds that face west.

I let myself lie back. The clouds move the way the swamp grass does, their motion waxing and waning with the wind. I am the fourth of the five of us to finally settle near water. What do children do who grow up and do not have a Wood Lake to come home to? I do not mean children who never get to move back to Wood Lake, but what do children do who never had Wood Lake, never had a place where the wind took over time and only the sun, by its setting, brought you home again?

NO ONE really lived on Wood Lake. It was small and surrounded by swamp, the way Mud Lake is. There was no shore anywhere, no swimming beaches, no boat landings. The tall grasses and crumbling woods were outer space to us. No matter how far we went, we did not come to the end. Some sense kept us from looking too far. We mapped out territories and kept to them.

Patty and I staked a claim one summer on the west shore of the nearest bay. We were married. A fallen oak tree was our home. It stretched out in the swamp grass many times farther than we were tall, and its branches that were as big as trees were the rooms of our house. We had a path down to the edge of the lake. The water-soaked soil squooshed and bubbled as we walked along, yielding to the weight of our bodies that carried so little weight elsewhere in the world.

The shore was barely distinguishable from the water, but we knelt there anyway, soaking up the black muck that is the basis of life, and with sticks we dug for snails and with twigs we gutted their shells and in a tin can mixed the hapless creatures with water and algae and hung the stew pot from a forked branch over a wigwam of twigs that we did not even want to light since we had once stood on the crest of the hill that tumbles down to the swamp and watched a fire that was red and orange and black swallow all of the grasses, leaving naked our safe harbor.

We found a dead mouse. Brought a white square of cloth from home to wrap it in. Placed it in the cradle of a tree hollow that was high enough so it was hard to reach. Took it out over and over again, holding it in our open palms, pulling back the swaddle, stroking its fur, talking to it.

It was our first death.

CROOKETY LANE followed the southwest curve of the south bay of Wood Lake, but at a respectable distance. It did not lead anywhere, except away from 73rd Street. It was narrow, and rutted. The dirt felt good underfoot, different than the real streets.

To the right as you walked there from home, the grasses leaped up and shielded the lake. You could barely see the branches of Patty's and my tree home. To the left, the ground lifted away from the road, washed out at first, but then nailed in place by virgin hardwoods.

Those trees were the magnet. Roots as big as a man's leg reached out from the tree bases before they dove underground. We sat on them the way we sat on Papa Jack's knees. And the crotches between the legs were open: dark triangular portals to the earth. The brave ones stuck their hands in there.

Bunny holes, we called them.

WOOD LAKE is dried up now, the cold waves of water that rocked wild ducks given way to ground. It is a sanctuary, surrounded entirely by chain link fencing, and paths and wooden boardwalks dissect the stands of tall grasses where birds still homestead. I park my car several blocks from what was once home and slip through the "Z" opening in the fence.

I stop where the path crosses behind Kimm's house. If I move just right, I can see my house behind it, across the street. And here in the corner of Kimm's yard, right next to the fence, a swing set frame, so rusted red that it is almost back to ore.

Further around the curve of the bay where I once killed snails, the path forks and one branch aims for the heart of the lake. Water has not forgotten this spot, and I lift my feet up onto the boardwalk. I can hear the rub of shoes on the walk ahead of me, but because grass also remembers this place I cannot see who is there.

A bench to sit on. Grass brushes my shoulders. I tilt my head back, close my eyes and listen. Wind also has a base here. Patty's and my tree is gone. The rooms of a real house overlook that ground. And Crookety Lane is a real street, with paving and curbs and gutters and drains that shed water like tears into a concrete aquifer that hustles what might have been waves on a lake clear across town to a river that runs away as fast as it can to another state.

THE GIRL
ON THE PORCH

THE PORCH was on the east side of the house, abutted the east living room wall, its other three sides screened from the ceiling down about two-thirds of the way to the floor. The only entry was through a door to the right of the fireplace in the living room.

The floor of the porch was wood, and sloped away from the house, so rain water would flow toward and through the three horizontal slots along the east wall. I liked to lie on my stomach and peer through those little windows. They took the unwieldy canvas of the yard and put a twelve by three inch frame around it. Squirrels and kids and dogs would appear as though from nowhere, cross my field of vision, and disappear again, never knowing that for a moment they had been lifted out of time and space.

The porch itself was a refuge from the clock. Because there was no outside entrance, it was not a passageway into the house, and because you had to go through the living room to get to it, it was a sanctuary from the chaos of the kitchen.

The other kids were not interested in the porch. Grownups used it for long afternoons of droning conversation and in-jokes, or evenings after we went to bed. Then, from the upstairs window, you could see the light cast out on the dark grass, and you could hear the ripples of laughter that came to us as though across water.

I used the porch in the mornings, before anyone was up. Called from my bed by mourning doves called up by the sun, I would walk as though asleep down to the porch and curl up on the chaise lounge. For awhile I would listen, eyes open — woooo, woo, woo, woo . . . wooo, woo, woo, woo — then, as the sun laid shadows on the house wall inside the porch, I would sleep that fine sleep of early morning when the body is already rested and yields easily to dreams.

Mother liked to watch me there. How did I come to be behind her in this memory, watching her standing in the doorway between the house and the porch, arms extended, palms flat on the door frame, watching me?

I LIKED being on the porch with the adults, even though I did not understand why they laughed when they did, or why they laughed at me when they did. They bounced gently in their metal tube chairs with the shell shaped backs, talking to each other with the familiarity of children. I would lie on the chaise, sometimes listening, sometimes staring at the Mexican straw hat tacked to the house wall. Its head piece was normal, but it had a four foot diameter brim spread out like a twirling skirt, jagged roads of pink straw woven through it. I tried to follow them around and around but never got to the crown. And I imagined wearing it, dancing in it, spinning so fast that the brim stood all the way out.

One fall I biked home from school every day for lunch, and Mother and I ate on the porch. The high, noon sun rattled in the leaves of the big hardwood that held its branches out toward us and filtered light down onto us like rain. I loved being alone there with my mother. She had lunch ready and brought it out on a little tray, and we ate quietly and quickly because I had to get back on my bicycle and pump the two dozen blocks back to the brown brick school, where the other children would be just coming in from the flat heat of the playground.

And I sat on the porch once with Aunt Maude. I do not know how she was related to us. I loved her. She made clothes for my baby doll, a blue calico print dress with ruffles at the hems of the sleeves and the skirt, and a white cotton slip with a thin band of lace around the yoke.

Aunt Maude loved me. She was heavy and warm and her hair was as white as an angel's. When we sat on the porch she said "I had a daughter once." When my Andrew was born, I went to her, and suckled him, and she watched.

RICHFIELD

IN THE 1940s and '50s, Richfield was a fresh suburb clinging to the south skirt of Minneapolis, north-south avenues laid out alphabetically, Aldrich, Bryant, Colfax, Dupont, Emerson, Fremont, Girard, and dissected east to west numerically, 73rd, 74th, 75th. In our neighborhood, double lots were held in place by unique houses. These in turn were held in place by mature oak trees and maples and elms. This bit was not farmed or logged before the city got to it. Maybe it was grazed. I like to think of cows meandering along self-made paths, and at night, deer foraging for acorns.

I liked the acorns myself. Sitting on the front lawn while Dad worked there, I would rummage in the grass, collect a handful with their little tufted hats, peel them and eat them. "You'll turn into a squirrel," Dad said, and one afternoon I went alone to my chaise on the porch and fell into a deep afternoon sleep and dreamt I was a squirrel eating acorns. When I woke it was dusk. I had missed dinner, and the after dinner games were just closing down across the street in Kimm's yard. Still in a trance, I ate the bit of food Mother warmed up for me and then nested again in my bed, curled into myself.

THE KIMM kids had to pick a pail of weeds each after dinner before they could play. By the time they were done, almost everyone was in their yard. It was the best one for Draw the Frying Pan, our version of Hide and Seek, because it stood on top of the hill leading down to the lake, and no driveways or streets interrupted passage into the yards on either side. The game started in the front where an oak tree bigger around than the joined arms of many children served as base. The person who was It had to count to 100 and then draw a frying pan on the tree, and put in the bacon and eggs and cook them before they could call out "Ready or not, here I come."

This one game transcended the boundaries of age that otherwise dictated our playmates. Newcomers were always It, and being little or younger did not save you from the ferocious honesty of the players. I was often late, and I hated the taunting — "cucumbers it — cucumbers it!" and one time said so and burned redder than a dogwood switch in spring when they laughed and laughed and Gretchen finally told me why.

The whole neighborhood was our family. The closer the house to ours, the closer the knit. I understand now that the children in the houses at the rim of my circle were at the center of their own circles, and I was on their rims, but at the time, all directions went out from me.

I was in the center too of the age wheel. An older sister and brother, a younger sister and brother. Across Emerson, Lottielee one year older, Diane, one year younger. Next door, Patty older, Julie younger. Across 73rd, two Kimms older, two Kimms younger.

Diane was my first steadfast playmate. Then Patty. Then Lottielee. These liaisons lasted years each. Lottielee, Lee now, is still within arms' reach.

MARGARET MARY Walters lived two doors down from Kimm's. She was Nicky's age, I think — four years my younger? I didn't play with her, but I liked to visit her mother, who loved me, and called me her petunia — "a lonely little petunia in an onion patch," she would sing. I was afraid of Pauly, Margaret Mary's older brother, Gretchen's age, who liked to pick me up and try to put me in the clothes' chute, but it was worth facing him to visit "Aunt Catherine."

The Walters were Catholic. Dad said so. It mattered, but he liked them anyway. Papa Jack was death on Catholics. He told me why once, or did my Dad tell me? When he was a boy, Papa Jack had gone to a ball game. A priest was behind him in line and told Jack he should put that money in the offering at church, and then the priest got in to the game free. What other angers, I wonder, swarmed into that moment of injustice and burst into a lifelong hate?

I didn't understand the thing about Catholics, but I did understand that it had something to do with Mr. Walters being in the living room. Lottielee and I were playing in my yard one day, by the swing set. We had dishes, or tools and were digging something. "What if Margaret Mary comes over?" Lee worried. "What if she wants us to look at her Dad?"

What if? And then Margaret Mary came out of her house and crossed the street and cut across Cochran's yard next to us and, skipping her way toward us, hollered "Want to come see my Dad? He's dead ya know."

Lottielee disappeared. It was my yard, and there was Margaret Mary, five years old, wanting me to come with her.

I went. The living room was dark. Halfway across it, in the imaginary line between it and the dining room, was the coffin. Was the lid up? I think so, but in my memory the box is filled with haze.

"Aren't you going to pray?"

"What for?"

"So he will go to heaven."

She showed me how to kneel on the velvet board and I did, but I did not pray.

How long was it after that that my mother's father died? Papa W. B. — Papa Double Bubble Gum, because he always had some in his pockets. After the funeral, when everyone was in the house eating from the hundreds of dishes of food that appeared the way grass greens after rain, I went out and sat cross legged in the center of the three pine trees in the side yard. They rose out of the ground around me like women with copious green skirts. What is it like to be dead, I wondered? Would you miss yourself? Would you be full of sorrow, crying into yourself, unable to be comforted?

No. I decided that if you were dead, you would not know it, so you would not feel bad about it. There was nothing I had to do. Once I was dead, I would not care that I was.

Now that was taken care of, I said to myself, as I pushed out through the stiff skirts of the trees.

I knew I was lying.

Form 39 4m 5-42 dp

THE SWEDISH HOSPITAL
MINNEAPOLIS, MINNESOTA

Baby *Girl Hauser*

Born at 5 55 p.m. 12-24-42

Antenatal Observations

Labor: Mother *Normal*

Postnatal Observations: Mother

Baby's Health Record

Physical Examination

Cord *off*   Eyes *o.k*   Skin *o.k*

Weight 7# 13 oz   Birth

Minimum 7# 8oz   Date 12-26-42

Dismissal 7# 13 oz   Date 1-2-43

Amount oz 2½ to 3   Breast Milk   Date

Bleeding Time   Date

Coagulation Time   Date

Length 20½ inches

FORM 46

THE SWEDISH HOSPITAL

BABY *Girl Hauser*   WEIGHT 7# 13oz   SEX *Female*

DOCTOR *Drs. Linner- Dunlap*   DATE 12-24-42

BABY'S FEET

LEFT   RIGHT

MOTHER'S THUMB

LEFT   RIGHT

SIGNED *B. Jenkins*

BABY GIRL HAUSER

The Swedish Hospital
Minneapolis, Minnesota

Baby Girl Hauser
Born at 5:55 p.m. 12-24-42
Labor: Mother Normal
Cord off   Eyes ok   Skin ok
Weight 7# 13 oz
Minimum 7# 8 oz   Date 12-26-42
Dismissal 7# 13 oz   Date 1-2-43
Length 20 inches

The seven by seven inch white form has no signature. The notations are made in four different shades of blue fountain pen ink. Many of the items are left blank.

There is a second form, smaller and folded inside the first, on heavier beige paper:

The Swedish Hospital

Baby Girl Hauser   Weight 7# 13 oz   Sex Female
Doctor Drs. Linner-Dunlap   Date 12-24-42
Baby's Feet
                    Left   Right

            Mother's Thumb
Left   Right

                    Signed B. Jenkins

29

I MAKE a fist with my hand, the way we did as kids, to make baby feet on frosted winter windows. You hold the fist, warm blooded, little finger side against the cold glass. When you lift it away, it leaves a print, left hand for left foot, right hand for right foot. To make the toes, you bunch your fingers and thumb together and place the tips above the ball of the foot, right hand for right foot, left hand for left foot.

I did not know how perfect the size was. At forty-seven my fist just overlaps my newborn foot. And my thumb prints fit my mother's.

How was it for her to give birth? Was that when anesthesia was popular, or did she lift her head as mine emerged through the perineal gate and watch me slide into air? How long did she labor? Where was my father?

When on the 24th did she begin to know that I would be born? In the morning when she got up, while Gretchen and Brooks ate their breakfast, did she lean back against the kitchen cupboard while the first hands of a contraction grew in the small of her back and then reached long fingers around to the front of her basket of flesh?

Who took care of my brother and sister? And when did she call my father at work? It was Christmas Eve. Was the store open? Maybe he was home all day, coming to her now and then, standing behind her, putting his arms all the way around to her front, squeezing her just a little so she would know he was there.

When did they go to the hospital and what did she think as she lay there, the strap of muscles around her uterus working, working, doing its job, releasing me from her body, releasing her body from mine?

Did I suckle? Did I feel the cold air of earth waft over my naked body as I took my first journey from her perineum to her breast, my mouth already seeking ground?

She must have smiled then, drawing her hand around my head.

When did they name me? Susan was probably picked before-hand. What was my middle name to be before I was born on Christmas Eve? Susan Carol, for Christmas song, Mother told me once.

COUNTING BACK from Christmas Eve, I come nine months earlier to mid March, by coincidence, the month I am writing in. The month of my conception. The week of the vernal equinox. Cusp between winter and spring. Cusp between not being and being.

An ovum tumbles down the chute toward the uterine swamp. The children are in bed. There is time left in the evening, but Howard and Louise let themselves be drawn too toward sleep.

They undress themselves, get into the bed from opposite sides. They kiss good night. Then keep on kissing. Her nipples, brown from suckling, lift from their dry beds and she parts her legs and takes his penis into her, into the river bed that this month will not flow with menstrual blood. He rocks on the pelvic cradle where I will rock. Her perineum engorges, then pumps itself dry and he feels the tide of her body ebbing and he lifts himself then a little more and also crests and semen fills her vagina and the little cup at the top of the vagina and seeps through the cervical door and mingles with the swamp waters of the uterus.

The ovum drifts in the uterine currents; one sperm bumps into it. Intercourse takes place again.

It could have happened like that.

JANUARY 2, 1943 — the day I came home from the hospital. It is not until I see that on the hospital record that I realize I did not experience the year 1942.

My sense of bearing shifts a little. The year I have always counted from is not really mine. I belong to 1943 — one of those odd numbered years between the births of myself and most of my siblings: Brooks-1940, me-1942, Karen-1944, Nick-1946. Gretchen was born in '37 — a different decade. Three years an only child. The only one to have her own room.

I begin to feel as though I have lost a year of my life, as though I had been lying when I claimed association with 1942. I had always liked the way the numbers fell out: 12/24/42: 12 is half of 24; 42 is 24 reversed.

Another note on the hospital record rankles: *Amount:* oz. 2 1/2 to 3..... *Breast Milk* ....

Was I bottle fed? Was that the amount of breast milk calculated by weighing me before and after nursing? I thought Mother nursed us all. When I was suckling Andrew in the privacy of the living room at Dad's house, he came in and watched me. When I stopped he said "The dairy bar is closed. That's what your mother always said."

When Dad was dying, I slept with him one night in the king size bed, so his wife Lue could sleep all night just one night. I thought we should put a pad on the floor and I would sleep there, but Lue said no, he does not move, and she was right. His skin clad skeleton stayed where we put it. Only his legs climbed each other, as though he were working his way up a stairway.

I did not sleep well. Had a waking dream of suckling my father, cradling him at my breast. How I wanted to hold him, to make him fit in my arms.

Part Two

SUN BATH

THE SKY is bright. No wind. I do not want to settle down to writing. Instead I take the foam pad out onto the deck, take off my clothes and lie down on it.

The two inch thick mattress is just a little wider than my body, and just a little longer. I made it years ago, and have carried it with me since then. Like a child's kindergarten rug, I pull it out for quick naps. The brushed cotton cover is familiar. Today it is also warm with the sun, and is soft against my buttocks and back.

I let my eyes graze across the great bowl of the sky. There are no clouds and, as though the emptiness is too much to bear, I begin to see into the little ocean of water that floats across my eyeballs. Motes of dust and debris come into focus, churning around as though by will.

The air around me is also filled with motion. Because I am lying so still, birds do not see me. They cross in front of me and over me, and come from behind me, pumping with their wings against the gravity that pulls at all of us.

I can hear the air repeatedly crushed against their feathers, a soft sort of beating sound, whoosh, whoosh. From the hillside, I also hear leaves, first yielding to, then resisting the breeze.

Then I close my eyes. The sun still enters, muted through my eyelids, and stronger through my skin. I am a little embarrassed to like so much the feel of it on my breasts, and my groin. I move my hands from my sides to my chest, my palms over my nipples, my fingers stretching out to overlay the bags of flesh. Now I can feel the sun twice, on the breasts themselves, and again on the insides of my hands.

I remember the first time I masturbated. I was in my late twenties. I had two children, had been married and making love for ten years. I had never made love to myself.

I move one hand, my right hand, down to my pubic hairs and with my middle finger finesse back the curls, the labia, settle against the right hand side of the fleshy hood of the clitoris. My buttocks and hips pull up in cooperation. I breathe deeply in, slowly out. I open my eyes and the blue of the sky fills my brain.

It has taken years to take time with this. I used to work quickly. Orgasm was the goal. Sometimes it still is, when I am exhausted and the energy of the day is caught up in my glands and I want to wring them dry. The pulsations then are quick and staccato. One last thing done — this one just for me. Sleep comes.

Today I do not want to sleep. I want to keep my consciousness. I want to walk inside my body the way I walk along a forest path. Small things then make me happy — anemone blooming through handfuls of dried leaves, and all the while birds climbing the trees around me.

With my left hand, I press down on my left breast. My nipple lifts out of its bed and I respond, moving my palm the way an infant moves its lips, coaxing the nipple further out. This I feel in my groin. I separate again labia that have settled back against each other and draw my finger from the base of the clitoral cloak up to the open top of the hood. The clitoris itself begins to grow and take shape, a thimble of nerves.

I close my eyes again, and travel with the sensation from nipple to groin. There does not seem to be a road. There is the one point, then the other. In between is sky.

It is the diffuse sky of the orgasm itself, when all that is focused and tethered loses its grip and becomes airborne. Another charge leaps from nipple to clitoris. The vulva receives this the way water takes in a stone dropped from well above the surface. Concentric waves radiate out, breaking into the vagina, the pelvis, the rectum.

I move both of my hands to my belly. It is soft and fleshy, the way it is just after a baby is born. The arousing wake has spent itself and I am aware of the steady heat of the sun distributed evenly over my entire body.

I LIKED being pregnant. And I liked breast feeding my babies. It was my first sustained and selfish sensual experience. It felt good, both in my breasts and in my groin. The baby felt good in my arms. Both of us were doing what we were supposed to be doing. It was simple.

Much simpler than sex. I still don't have that figured out, maybe because I was so slow to pick up on it. I didn't see it around me as a child, although surely it was there. My mother told me about it, about sperm swimming to meet ova. There was, of course, no mention of vaginas or penises. I thought, how marvelous — and imagined these little tiny wisps emanating from the man's body, wagging themselves across the sheets, and being absorbed into the woman's body.

"Where does the baby come out?" I asked.

"Where do you think?" my mother replied.

Why didn't I try to make better sense of it, ask more questions, look it up in a book? I did not know about male erections until I held one in my hand. Before that, the only penis I saw was about five years old, on a nephew. And it wasn't until after I had intercourse that I could find the hole referred to in the tampon instruction sheets.

Being pregnant helped. I had books by then. Knew when the baby's fingernails were developing. But I still did not think about my own body. The baby would come out the way it had gotten in. All I had to do was wait.

Looking back, I am in awe of how consistent my behavior is, even though I was so often unconscious. I did not extrapolate meaning from action. There was only event. Still, some part of me knew what was going on, sent me in the right direction. When I was thirteen, I read an article in the newspaper about a doctor who taught self-hypnosis for childbirth. I had heard about birth and pain. I had heard that drugs were bad. I cut the article out, put it in my jewelry box.

Eight years later, I excavated it, found the doctor, learned self-hypnosis. Used it for both of my deliveries. Still did not know what I was doing.

I did know that I was missing something, though. Now I know that I had not yet Come of Age, even though I was married, had children, ran a household. I was still just piecing together a script from the scenes and backdrops of home. I did not look up and wonder about the horizon.

Then one day, I did. I went back to school. I got divorced. I learned to masturbate.

I OPEN my eyes again. This time I will get serious. My clitoris has slipped back into its case, but comes out willingly at first touch. With my left hand, I hold back the labia majora, can feel the sun on the labia minora. I move my right middle finger in circles on the outside of the cloak, pull my hips up, let them down, then move to finer, inner muscles — contract my rectum. Release. This excites the vaginal muscles, harder to awaken. Now I pull on them, first in the long barrel, then toward the top, concentrating there on the shy bands that have to be coaxed into action.

Short breaths in, long breaths out, flattening my stomach, emptying my vagina. Breathing in now long, low and deep, I infuse my pelvis with air. My vagina opens the way the sky opens for birds.

An orgasm is different with an empty vagina. The walls brush on themselves as they suck in and let out as gently as a baby's lips at breast. The rectum contracts obviously, a firm hand, a finishing touch. Sometimes the uterus also gasps. I blink my eyes. First sky comes into focus. Then sound returns. I put my hands back on my breasts. Close my eyes again. The last of the waves wash through my thighs.

THIS
I WOULD DO

THE WINDOWS of the room he designed himself opened out onto the tops of the Florida orange trees. He left as much of the grove intact as possible, taking only enough space for the house, a bit of yard front and back, and an alley of grass leading like a rope from the house down to the lake.

This morning the sky and the water are both utterly blue and utterly calm. I stand for awhile in the window and look out. To my left and behind me, I hear his breathing that is at last quiet. The treetops are at the level of my feet and I can see down into the branches and there I can see the birds moving about, fussing at the thimbles of fruit.

Because it is morning and because the room faces west, heat that seems to rise from the ground does not yet penetrate this wall of glass. Later in the day, when it clearly comes from above, we will drop the blinds, stopping it short.

Later in this day, it will not matter. Before noon, the breathing will stop. I know that, as I sit down in the chair at the head of the bed. His bed. Not the hospital bed he is sleeping in now, tucked into the little ell that was supposed to hold a wood stove one day, a Minnesota back-home touch. His real bed. The one he slept in until last night, when we could no longer turn him and lift him on his own mattress without hurting him.

I lean back in my chair, propping my feet on the bed, crossing them at the ankles, the way Dad had done so often the last few days, as though he had just come in from work, and was settling down to let the effort of the day precipitate out. It was a casual gesture, incongruous.

We all knew we were here to help Dad die. Even Dad knew. When I arrived, he asked when I was going back.

"I'm not going back. I'm here to stay."

He had been in bed for several days. The next day he asked me, "Is this trip fatal?"

I had promised myself that I would not lie. I hedged: "I will ask the doctor."

And the next day I knelt beside the bed and leaned against it and took his hand and tried to not cry but I cried and cried and told him this time he would not get better. The regular treatments would no longer reverse the symptoms. There was a different one they could do, but it would hurt, and would not make him better, even for awhile. It would only keep him this way longer.

I held his hand tighter, but he did not squeeze back. The tumor in his brain had pinched off control of his arms. Neither did his eyes respond. In just one week, his vision had melted away.

I asked him not to leave us yet. "We have more time. We have things to say."

"All right."

Oh, this is what I did not have with Aaron. When I got to him on the pavement, he was already gone. His eyes were open, fixed on the sky. My finger to his wrist, I could feel his heart beating in knotted threads. I leaned down and put my lips to his ear, asked him to stay. Asked him to stay.

"Don't try to pick him up. Don't move him." Voices kept coming down to me.

We did not know how grey it was for Dad. We announced ourselves when we came in, in case he confused our voices. Later, when we moved him to the hospital bed, and the nurses came, we reminded him that he was at home.

We had several days. I did not know about the mercy of a tumor in the brain. Yes, sentience slowly slipped away, but without pain. Some senses lingered. Coffee from a spoon tasted good. Nick brought in a TV for listening to the evening news, and during the day we played the radio, brought in from its post on top of the kitchen fridge.

And we sat in the chair by the side of the bed, my sisters and brothers and I, and talked to Dad, and told him stories about our lives.

As we had sat by our mother's hospital bed. But we were too young then to understand or to help. She wanted to go home to die. We did not know how to do it.

This time I was able to ask, "What are you thinking about?"

"Nothing."

Then, "I wonder if I did more bad than good."

They say that if you go down into a well in daytime and look up, you can see the stars.

I DID not know that it was such hard work to attend at death. I knew already about grief, because of Aaron, and I had been at other dyings, when I was a nurse's aide in the hospital. But there it was part of the shift.

This home death was different. Like a birthing. We moved together the way dragonflies cruise, working their little patch of air. We carried food in to Dad and sat close to him and fed him, moving our mouths when he moved his.

We eased sheets sad with the rub of his long skeleton out from under him and teased clean ones into place.

When tears flowed out of the artesian wells of our hearts, we brought our arms around each other in baskets of praise.

When my father no longer cared that he lay naked in front of us, we no longer cared.

I washed him.

He let me. I started with his face, moved down his arms, his torso. Skipped down to his legs, his feet. Took a deep breath. Returned to the lap of soft hairs, bathed the penis, from whence I had come.

WE GOT a commode for alongside the bed, then a urinal. The last night, I helped the nurse put in a catheter. Gretchen and I slept in Dad and Lue's bed. Lue slept downstairs. The previous night with Dad in their own bed had been her last one.

We woke and slept to Dad's rhythm, getting up to help the nurse turn and rub, then letting ourselves down again into the small glow of one shrouded lamp.

Lying there in the half-light between death and life, I actually felt lucky. I was helping my father die. It was physical work, like shoveling dirt or digging post holes. A labor. I felt strong.

Mother, this I would have done for you, had I known how.

Aaron, this I would have done for you had there been time.

Father, thank you.

CEREMONY

THE MALL courtyard was designed to look like a tropical garden. In fact, it did. Rangy *ficus* trees reached up to balconies that looked down on the main level. Ferns hung from railings, trailing their greeny trains. Philodendron crept around the bases of the *ficus* trunks. Palms held the spaces in between.

I sat behind one of the long tables arranged in a broad semi-circle around the outer edge of the courtyard space and facing the platform and podium that backed up against the glass elevator wall. The people who had been moving through the middle space were lined up now behind the tables, the overflow hanging over the railings of the balcony and of the zigzag stairway that came to rest directly across from the podium.

The other writers and I straightened the little stacks of books in front of us, then sat with our hands in our laps, trying to convince ourselves that it was all right if we did not win. It was, after all, a crazy little contest: the Minnesota Book Awards, a fledgling effort by libraries and bookstores to let the public know about its home state authors.

My family formed another semi-circle, this one around the back of my chair. Suddenly the man at the podium was reading the nominees in my category. I nodded my head at each one; dropped my head at the name I thought would win; shook my head at mine.

Then I felt my Aunt Marion lean in behind me. She pressed her stomach tightly against my back. Then she put her hands on my shoulders. Then she leaned tighter against me, her breasts bracketing my head, her hands spreading out over my shoulders. I leaned my head back against her and for a moment lost my vision as my dead mother, her sister, flowed through me, through Marion's breasts and hands into my shoulders, down through my chest and my torso and my pelvis and thighs and calves and grounding in my feet.

"Meant To Be..." the man behind the podium was saying. Marion turned her palms outward, releasing me, and I found myself in the middle of the courtyard. To my left I could hear Karen and Joe and Marion and Georgia crying and clapping and even yelling.

It was a long time later when Marion and I stood face to face, chest to chest, arms around backs and looked into each other's eyes. "That was Mother," I said.

"Yes."

MY MOTHER would like what I am doing now. When I was fifteen or sixteen and I had commented on something I had read, she said to me, "You could be a writer."

The notion did not interest me and would not for ten years or more. Reading is what I liked to do. I read novels, mostly those for young adult females. I liked the old ones best, *Girl of the Limberlost*, *Heidi*, *Little Women*. And I was faithful to my authors. If I liked one book, I read them all.

If someone wanted to find me, they knew where to look: "She's in her room again, reading." It was an accusation. There were not a lot of rules around our house, and reading was a good thing to do in the evening, or before going to bed, but it was not something to do during the day, when you could be outside, or at the very least doing something around the house.

I don't remember learning to read. I don't remember when I fell under the spell of words. I do remember that for quite awhile when my mother went downtown, she stopped at the fourth floor bookstore in Dayton's and bought me a book. That ended the summer I would read one in its entirety in one afternoon.

I was introduced to the public library. It was a long way on my bicycle, clear across Lyndale Avenue, the de facto dividing line between our neighborhood and the next. I didn't feel safe over there, but that's where the books were.

And I didn't like having to take the books back. Already I was a hoarder. There are still two books from that summer that I wish I had: one about a fourth story cupola, the other about a girl and her father and a fishing wharf. And I am sorry that I once gave away my complete twenty-two book set of *Cherry Ames, Nurse* novels. How nice that would feel on the living room shelf, next to the *Little House* books and *Hans Brinker*.

When we built the house at Spring Lake, one whole wall in Karen's and my bedroom was made into book shelves. I just remember that now, as I write.

I KEEP trying to jiggle my memories into a pattern. They hold for a minute, then, like the colored glass chips in a kaleidoscope, they move from their own weight and take another shape. I would like to do a portrait of my mother. Closing my eyes, I try to let one, a visual one, emerge, but it too will not hold still. Always she is in motion, down the stairs to the basement, down the hallway to the bedrooms. Did I never catch up to her?

Physically, she was about my height. Until she had had cancer for a couple of years, she was plump. She did not like that. Her hair was light brown. Her eyes hazel. She was patient with us kids, patient with my father. I only saw her cry twice. Once, in Richfield, a houseful of little kids. She was making dinner and she was crying. She was stirring something on the stove with a long wooden spoon and she cried and cried. I do not know why.

The second time was later, in the car, after visiting her father. I was in the back seat. It was dark. She ran across the lawn, threw herself into the front seat, said "He is dying, he is dying," and she cried and cried and we drove off down the black street.

She wore house dresses. And when she and Dad went out to dinner she dressed up and she wore perfume, "Toujours Moi," and she smelled so good. I liked to sit on the bed in her room and watch her dress — fix her hair, put on a lacy bra, a silky slip, and a dressy dress that she pulled on over her head and that fed itself down over her body like water over a falls. She stood then in front of the mirror and nudged the darts and seams into place and then put on earrings and a necklace and a bracelet and Dad came home from work and I got out of the way so he could change and then they left, happy, I think, to be together and alone.

I STOPPED reading novels when I got married. Maybe that is when I caught up to my mother. Suddenly, there was no time for books, and I didn't mind that. I had a husband and children and a household and I was flipping through the pages of my life as fast as the calendar would let me.

I wish I knew what knocked me off track. Why, at twenty-six, did I begin to get restless? Why not at twenty? Or forty? It is a classic coming-of-age story. Until then, I was my parents. After divorcing them, I divorced my husband. It took a lot more than one sentence to do it. It took a whole lot of words. I did not start reading again, but I did start writing. I liked the way it felt. An idea, a moment, a feeling nailed to the page. Made to hold still, forever.

Epilogue

NIGHT WASHES in the way it does in the summer, in the country. The wind ebbs to a breeze and then falls still. The sky fades, then darkens. Loon calls cross the water.

Sitting in the screen house, we stack our dinner plates in the center of the little table, put our elbows in their places, and let the conversation find its own way among the four of us.

Vivienne and Michael will be leaving soon. Not just for the evening, but forever. They will move to Ohio and they will not come back, even though they think they will.

The frogs begin to sing, and fireflies blink, first in the tall grass at the edge of the hill, then in the yard, then just outside the screens. Michael knows everything about them. He learned it when he was a child, and he learned how to catch them, too.

We watch him with his wine glass in hand as he skips down the dark yard and around the lilac hedge. When he comes back, he has captured three. They flit around inside the glass, bouncing off his palm that serves as lid.

Sitting down, he releases them on the table. For that moment, they are the only light we have.

AFTERMATH

*A Journey through Loss
and into Light*

THE NEST

I open the front
of the birdhouse box.

The wall that is a door
swings down on its hinges:

light from my world
enters the cave.

A corona of feathers
cups the nest.
I stick one finger
into the ring,
pull back the pinions

and hold my breath:

four mouths open,
taking me in.

Heat rises like love
from their tiny throats:

this is the cradle we all come from.

Outside the mother
leaps and cries in the lilacs:

she knows
what I know.

IT IS dusk as my car makes the last turn north, toward home. The tree shadows that for awhile flickered across this country road have melted into pavement.

Ahead of me and to the right, a black dart drops out of the trees then pulls itself again up into the sky. It is a pileated woodpecker. The underside of its two foot wing span is ribbed with white. Its ruby topknot catches the last bit of daylight. Pumping the way a child pumps a swing, it rises and falls, up and down, carrying itself across the road and into the woods on the other side.

I smile. "Thank you," I say out loud. Refreshed, I dare to wonder: can a child speak through a bird? Can the dead speak to us at all? It is an argument I have with myself, but the answer does not matter. This bird erupting from the forest comforts me.

CANOE

Herringbone
the wake undulates
behind the boat.

Weeds
scull to the surface.

Silence runs a cat's paw.

The sun is drawn out
through a hole
in the sky.

So many ways to dance.
So many ways to die.

AARON DIED when he was nine years old. He had been playing in the creek across the road. Coming home, he mounted his bicycle and rode it up and out of the ditch and in front of a pickup truck. He died there on the pavement.

In the mornings that spring, before he died, we watched a pair of pileated woodpeckers from our kitchen window as they hammered away at bug-ridden hardwoods. They were our birds. Some people call them god woodpeckers. The white darts on their faces echo the strong, white bill that is as long as a child's finger. They continued to visit after Aaron died. These woodpeckers, I told myself, were his guardians, his guides.

REDPOLL ON A BROKEN BRANCH

Slight as the memory
of last night's dream
you enter the frame of my window.

The blush on your chest
is too rosy for blood.
Your scarlet cap
too neat to be an accident.

Even the dangling limb
of the tree
takes on new meaning
in your presence.

In the dream
Aaron died again.
This time
it was a river
that swept him away,

his small bright face
becoming water.

What is the comfort
of a redpoll
in a tree?

Smaller
than a child's fist.

Tenacious in wind.

It grips a twig,
whets
its bill,

breaks into air
like a boy suddenly free
of his body.

AARON DIED fourteen years ago. Still, I am sometimes overtaken with his presence, as when the woodpecker greets me on my way home. Other times, I am overwhelmed by his absence. I see school busses all the time without reacting to them, then, without warning, one taps a dormant well of sorrow. I pull over to the side of the road until the shaking subsides.

After so many years, this sorrow is separate from Aaron. It is mine, not his. When the tears first came like that, unbidden and without warning, I was usually in the grocery store. I remember standing over the milk display, unable to move, tears washing over my consciousness.

What is it about grocery stores? Once when I was visiting my brother, a friend of his came upon us in the parking lot. The man cradled two sacks of groceries in his arms. "How are you?" Barb and Nick wanted to know. The man's eyes filled with water. His wife had died recently. "Shopping is so hard," he said.

A friend answers my query: shopping is a homely, little task — the gathering of food. We are alone with our thoughts in an anonymous place. The subconscious surfaces on a river of tears.

A DREAM I HAD ONCE

The meadow sleeps this morning.
No breeze or sound moves there.

It is as though the earth
has stopped for just this while.

There is snow still. Some.
And the lake is frozen yet.

But it is spring.
Old dreams have returned like crows.

This is the month
of your death.

You have been gone now
for as long as you
were here.

Yesterday
I dreamed I had
a son who died.

So now you are a dream
I had once.

So now you are a dream
that comes back
the way crows do,

declaring the sky.

TEAR WELLS have triggers set deep in the earth of our memory, below the line of awareness. One friend weeps at marching bands. Another at the crooked, tinkling tune of an ice cream cart. Neither one knows why. Weddings and graduations also open the trap door, pressed not by sorrow, but by overabundance: it takes water to float the mass of personal and primeval memory we each carry into ceremony.

When my father was dying and we cared for him at home, we joked about the artesian tear well. Stand too long in one spot, and it will out.

MOTHER AND SON

Stepping away from your wife,
you follow me
away from the bookcase,
put your hand
on my shoulder,
turn me around,
put your arms around me
and pull me close.

I let myself be drawn in,
and you hold me tighter.

How strong you are —
your arms locking me
into your chest.

My heart begins to shake
but you are not afraid.

I press my ear
to your ear.

You are crying too.
Aaron belonged
to both of us

and now his belongings,
the drawings
and books,
lie strewn on the floor
the way
he would leave them.

Your brother.
My son.
Never to be
more than nine years old

and now awash
in these ancient tears.

THE GRIEF when a parent dies is double. Grief for the loss of the mother or father, and grief for the loss of the children we were. The buffer between us and death is gone. Now it is time to turn around, to look back toward our own children. To stand between them and death, as we have always tried to, but with nothing between death and ourselves.

Gretchen balked at becoming a grandmother. It was a kind of grief, she said. She was no longer the primary parent. That was her son's job now. He was raising the children.

Christine's mother sold her childhood home. Christine went out east to help. "Talk about grief," she wrote to me. In a rented van she returned home with relics: dressers and chairs. Her own child was learning to walk, to talk. As he played in his childhood home, he erased her childhood.

Little lessons in grief.

TO FOLLOW HOME
for Andrew, my son

I watch you from the house
in your lean bones walking
to the end of the dock.

The heron that waits there
gives you your place.

Sitting on the bench
that your grandfather made,
you take your guitar,
a woman, into your arms
and begin your song.

The sun, clean circle,
lets itself down into the treeline,
pulling with it the day
we have spent together.

Back up the hill
my father too
moves away from me.

He already knows the poem
I begin to write:
morning and evening
he treads the grove,

laying out footprints
to follow home.

"THERE IS no greater loss than
the death of a child," people tell me. "It is something you cannot
know unless it has happened to you," they tell me. I do not agree. Is
this poem about the end of a relationship or the end of a life?

WOMAN SEEKING FLOWERS

The hyacinth is not up yet,
not speaking through the black earth.
It is waiting for the longer sun
that pulls us
like faith
into summer.

She replaces the leaves
that mumble against the wall,
returns to the house.

From there she counts the earth's turns
into light,
into dark,
into the small hours in between
which are neither bright nor dull.

It was not her fault.

Death is everywhere,
and from it springs birth.
Flowers from old seed.
Soil from trees.

But what
from the empty bed
that rattles here?

What will grow
in the black space?
Sorrow.
Anger.

Greed.

Yes, greed. She wants
more than she has a right to.
Flowers in winter.
Birth without death.
She wants the sleep of innocence
but wants to keep
the glow of her new sadness.

A stone it knocks
in the chambers
of her heart.

She wants it gone.
But will not let it go.

It is her fault.

This too breeds.
It tumbles stone.
Turns her dreams.
Stitches sorrow into silk.

And when enough seasons
have climbed and fallen,

when she has learned again
to sleep,

she goes to look for flowers.
The hyacinth is not up yet.
Is waiting for the longer sun.

Through the black earth
she hears it speak.

Like faith it pulls her
into summer.

A large lesson in metaphor. We can know each other's sorrow, if
we dare.

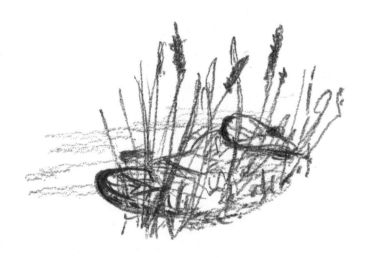

IN THE aftermath of death, time is a whirlpool, sucking us away from the moment of expiration. After Aaron died, I reviewed the accident over and over, looking for a flaw. Replay. Replay. Stop the bike at the edge of the road. Slow down the truck. It did not work. Aaron was dead.

"How can I help?" people would ask.

"If you cannot bring him back, don't ask me what you can do." That is what I wanted to scream.

Barb's words wrapped around me: "I am sorry you are so hurt."

HOW, LIKE THIS SPRING, SLOWLY

How, like this spring, slowly
I rise from the long steel winter.

Today driving past
the funeral home,

I saw myself walking
in that door. And I remembered

I did not dress you.
I am sorry for that.

I was glad
when you were born

to bare your torso,
feel each foot

and hand, to touch
your pouch,

to bring your wet mouth
to the river of my breast.

I told the man
I wanted to dress you.

He said no. I did not argue,
did not want to feel

your skin turned to stone,
to bone,

to not bend
in the water of my arms.

Like the spring slowly
I rise from the long steel winter.

In my dreams you are often
lost. In these words I
dress you now,
sweet Aaron,

your wildflower face,
these word-wings from my fingers
folding around
your willow bones.

Slow as spring
the spirit milk rises.

Bring your wet mouth.

DAWN DIED of breast cancer.
She was fifty. It is the utter aloneness, says Larry. Not loneliness.
Aloneness.

It is the existential angst. Existential angst. How perfect the
words are. The mind cannot really grasp them. That is the essence of
angst: it cannot be grasped any more than the absence of a person
can be held for long in the heart.

This is the existential angst: no one can stanch our pain, or undo
the deed.

This we can grasp: a pileated woodpecker pulsing through air.

DURING A PROLONGED ILLNESS

It is cool outside.
Autumn.
Not fall — not quick
like that.

Autumn.
Formal
in its turning.

Crows call
then, beating
their wings
against the sky,
move on.

Now it is quiet.
and I am glad,
though if I listen
I hear the breeze
coming this way
through the crisping leaves,

and from across the bay
a last loon whistle.

UNTITLED

I see my mother in the morning light,
sitting outside, the sun on her hair,
the lake at her feet, the water bright.

She leans back, watches birds in flight.
Shadows move across her face, along with the glare
of morning light.

She hates that fact: that black and white
come at once. I stare
at the lake, the water bright.

I am her age now, trying to write
her back into life, daring
to see her in morning light,

to take away titles: wife
and mother; what woman there,
the lake at her feet, the water, bright?

Hands on her belly, sun on her breasts, ignited
by cancer, she flares
in the morning light,
enters the lake at her feet. The water burns bright.

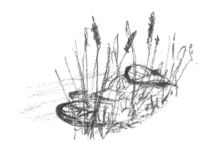

"THE SMALL hours in between light and dark, which are neither bright, nor dull." They came daily. Life lost its distinctions. Fear filled the void. I knew that the dead could not come back, but it had not mattered before. Even when my mother died too young, I did not think to ask for her back.

This was different. In the swell of grief, all I could think of to change the way I felt was for Aaron to be back. The momentum of our life together kept me rolling along for days and weeks and even months.

Grief became tangled with guilt: how could I live when Aaron did not? I was ashamed. And then I was ashamed that it mattered how I felt. Now I was grieving more for myself than for my son. Was there no damping my ego?

SONG

for Aaron

This window above my desk
faces north
and has given
to the winter sun
glass daffodils.

On the south wall of the house
we planted bulbs.
Their lips wait
for soil-webbed crystals
to drop into water.

I have hung bells
on the tree
by the back door.

Everywhere,
I leave notes for you.

THIS WOMAN

This woman thinks she is not beautiful.
Thinks the fold of anger in her heart
is truth.

She looks in the mirror. Cries.

I BEGAN to try to understand the fear that lit both my days and my nights. Again it was an absence, not a presence, that was causing the pain: I had no sense of well-being.

I began to attend to moments of pleasure: hepatica in the spring woods; candy made from wild ginger; a pinwheel from the dime store.

In flashes of light, I began to see how blind I had been in my grief. The people around me who loved me came into focus. My husband, who grieved; my other son, who grieved. Karen, who grieved for me as well as for Aaron. I had not seen their sorrow. When her sister died, a friend said, "my mother had all the grieving rights."

It is something to grieve over: there are things we cannot do for each other, no matter how much we love.

HARVEST ALMS

What do these children
know of the dead,

of the light
that leaps out
into the dark

through the gouged eyes
of a simple fruit.

They have come for candy.

Give it to them.

THERE IS a book called *Bitter, Bitter Tears,* by Paul Rosenblatt. It is about patterns of grief as revealed through nineteenth century diary entries. It suggests that grief work is not something we do for awhile and then it is done. It is something we keep doing throughout our lives. When reminders of the lost person appear to us, grief bubbles up the way a spring does in the wilds.

My husband and I made a pact early on. When Aaron slipped into our thoughts, we would say so. We would complain about him and laugh at him and laugh with him. We would not let every encounter with his memory be tainted with the little moment of his life that was his death.

BIRTHDAY

The day is perfect. The kind
a poet would write about,
the sky cerulean — a word
that means sky-blue
but says it better because
of the sound.

Ce-ru-le-an.
Cerulean.

I walk across the field
chanting.
The sky is cerulean.
The sky was cerulean the day
you were born. This day.

Cerulean.
Cerulean.

Now it begins to have
a different sound.
Cerulean.
Like an ancient name.
A character in a book.

Walking still, I come to the tree
that we call yours.
I fold back the leaves
that have gathered themselves
around its base.

Yes. The initials are there:
AA. For Aaron.

And in the root-hollow
the small things
we have brought here —
a crystal drawer knob.
A little round tin box.

The dead do not use toys.
But we think you would like this place.
I add today the barrette
from my hair.
Then sit on a log.
Then lie down on the forest floor
and look up into the cerulean sky.

SOMETIMES WE can feel the presence of the dead. Christine's sister colludes with her. And once my mother came at night to visit me. I felt her at the foot of the stairs, and she came all the way up to the doorway to my room. By this time I was awake. I stopped her there. I was afraid if I let her any closer, afraid that if I let myself partake of her consciousness, that I would be dead.

I was younger then, but old enough to have forgotten how to daydream. When I was little, I was always in trouble for daydreaming. I would just go somewhere else, and not know I had been there until I came back. Now I am learning to do it again.

THE DEER BEDS
for Aaron 1966-1976

In the field
south of the house
deer have been sleeping.

We do not see them,
do not hear them,

because we are so human,
we do not
smell them.

They come at night
in the country dark

and curl themselves
like kittens
into balls
of hide and bone.

The weight
of their bodies
crushes
the grass.

In the morning,
before we are up,
they rise
the way children try to
from angel beds
in the snow —
leaving no trace
of their exit.

Today,
your birthday,
I walk out
into the field
south of the house.

This bed
is fresh — it has
no frost, no dew.

I sit
in the warmth
of its circle.

You enter
my body.

GATHERING TIME
Essays from a Womanly Life

CONTENTS

DOWN
TO THE CITIES

BEMIDJI AIR flight 101 is cleared for landing at Minneapolis-St. Paul International Airport. The pilot does not tell us so. I hear it straight from air traffic control. Bleep. Squirch. "That 747's gonna hold back. Come on in in front of him." I break one of my own rules and look out the window, toward Wisconsin. The 747 does look like it's holding back. It seems not to move, the way a tornado looks when it's coming toward you. Our little Volkswagen of a plane hangs a right and the six of us, five passengers and a pilot, head for the ground. I tighten my grip on my pencil and force my eyes to focus on the "Across" clues on my crossword puzzle. It helps me keep the scream silent.

When we do touch down, my sigh of relief is audible. Maybe if I flew to "the Cities" more than once or twice a year, I would get used it. But now that I am on the ground, there are other worries. I have to find a cab to take me downtown.

It was a lot easier when I was a girl in Richfield, in the '50s. I just got in the car with Mom. She took 73rd Street over to Lyndale South, turned left and kept going until we got to the bottleneck where Hennepin and Lyndale crossed. Since we had to shoot right through the middle to switch over to Hennepin, it was probably not easier for my mother than bringing a commuter plane into the airport is now, but I didn't notice. I was busy counting the swans on the pond in Loring Park.

My mother died a long time ago. My driver today is from Afghanistan and he takes credit cards. This always happens to me when I come down to the Cities. I am startled, amazed by the ways technology is applied. A credit card machine in a car. The last time I was here I went to use the hand drier in a public bathroom. Instead of being mounted on the wall, it was inset. There was no "on" button. I followed the directions: "Insert hands." I stuck my fists into the hole in the wall. The air came on. I pulled them out. The air turned off.

It isn't such a big deal, really. It's just that a trick is never missed. If there is a way to make it quicker or simpler, then it is done. We talk about that up north. "Hey, if he wanted to, a fella could ...." But nobody wants to.

I am almost as afraid to look out the windows of the cab as I am the airplane. For a moment, I even believe that I was safer at 5,000 feet than I am in three lanes one way on the ground. I lean with the cab as we take the curve onto I-35. The Minneapolis skyline heaves into sight. The only building I recognize by name is the IDS. I could recognize the crown on the telephone building, and the clock on the court house, but they no longer command skyline status. Neither does the Foshay Tower. It *was* the skyline when I was a kid. We felt very brave the time we went up to its lookout deck. We did not imagine the shadows that would one day fall across it.

The cabbie double parks in front of a renovated warehouse on First Avenue North, a block my mother wouldn't have been caught dead on, and slings my wheeled carry on bag up onto the sidewalk. I take it by the leash and it begrudgingly follows me into the building, its plastic wheels screaming on the tile floor.

Of course everyone turns to look. "I grew up here," I want to yell, "I really do belong here." It wouldn't help. There is something about the way we northerners dress that gives us away no matter how much we try to keep up. And I have quit offering explanations in the elevator when folks say to each other "Do you smell bacon?" It's none of their business that I heat with wood, or that there is no way to rid clothes of smoke auras.

My first appointment, on business, goes well. I will have time for some shopping before my next one, about eight blocks away. My four wheeled friend and I hit the sidewalk.

Happily, the singing of my wheels no longer highlights my presence. The din of the city drowns it out. I make the two block hike over to the Nicollet Mall and turn right. As I walk, I fish my appointment book out of my purse. The last page in it has my Cities' list. These are things I cannot get in Bemidji. Kosher salt for making soft pretzels, and canned coconut. They will have to wait until I get to a grocery. Barrettes. The kind that hold really long hair in a knot. The only place I could get them for years was at the downtown dime store. The last time I was here they didn't have them. I'm hoping. ...

Following the construction ropes, I crisscross the mall and enter Woolworth's through the IDS lobby. My bag is still with me, catching on counter corners and other people's shopping bags. There are no good barrettes. There are people. Too many people, and they are moving too fast.

I nudge my way back out to the street, thinking I will take a good, deep breath there. The dust in the air is palpable and has taste. Might as well be in the wake of a log truck on a dirt road. I cross over to Dayton's, the store I grew up in. I have forgotten that I have a caboose, and my bag gets caught in the revolving door. My mother always did hate those things.

What do I want in Dayton's? Everything. And how do people make all these choices anyway? At home, if I want a tea kettle, I go to the hardware store and buy the tea kettle. No color decisions. No size decisions. No style decisions. I escape to the street again, this time through a side door, and park myself and my bag against the wall of a building. Just because I'm in the Cities doesn't mean I have to shop. So what if I get to my doctor's appointment way too early. I look up and around for the familiar scroll work on the Medical Arts Building. It is just across the street from where I am standing. Miraculous. It calls to me with the grace of a cathedral.

After two false entries into street side shops, I find the door into the lobby. My bag hums musically on the granite floor. I am the only person going in, and when I get to the main hallway, only a few people meander past. A couple of others sit on a bench. One person stands in front of the floor directory, drawing his finger down the long list. I too look for my place.

Then I am alone in front of the elevators. For the first time in hours I take in and let out a slow, deep breath. I even close my eyes. The last time I was in this building was more than twenty years ago. I was pregnant and my doctor's office was here. Before that I used to come with my mother, to see my orthodontist, and before that our pediatrician.

My eyes respond to the bong of the elevator call, so much more resonant than the electronic pings we hear on airplanes. I step into the car — my grandmother called the elevator a car. It is golden with brass. I lean against the soft rubbed rail. The doors whisper closed, the basket lifts, and I feel like I am being carried home.

My faithful bag comes with me out of the elevator. I take another long, deep breath and move slowly along the hall. The mail slot is still there, the brass mouth opening into a glass fronted chute that drops from the top floor to the first. My sisters and I used to stand there and watch, hoping someone on a floor above would mail a letter so we could watch it plummet past us.

I find my doctor's office and get the key to the ladies' room. I hang out there awhile. The window opens and is open. I shove it up a little more and lean out. I wonder if there is another building in this city where you can actually put your elbows on the window sill and look down onto the street.

This appointment goes well, too. I have only good news to take home with me, but I am a long way yet from the air taxi back to the woods. Tonight I will stay with friends, tomorrow more appointments. Today I have been downtown for almost six hours. Only for the last two, in Medical Arts, has it seemed like "downtown," a tag that has some of the warmth of "home town."

Trailing my sagging sack of possessions behind me, I reluctantly reenter the elevator and initiate the controlled fall back to the ground floor. There I stop someone and ask what is the best way to get a cab.

There are direct phone lines in the entry. Just pick up the one of my choice, and someone will answer. They are on the inside wall. I stare at the trio: blue for Blue and White, red for Red and White, yellow for Yellow. I find myself trying to make a rational decision about which one is best. No way to know. How shall I decide? The only values in front of me are color. I'm too tired for red or yellow. Blue is soothing. The color of sky, or water.

I pick up the phone. There is no dial wheel. Before I can wonder what to do next, a voice asks me where I am. I tell him where the phone is. That's all he needs. "Just wait. We'll be there."

There is a bench outside. I slump down onto it, stow my bag between my knees. Across from me, on the curb, are four mailboxes. Each one has a sign on it. Metered Mail. Express Mail. Stamped Mail. Larger Than Letters. The writer in me balks. What is "larger than letters" that would go in a letter box? Letters larger than letters?

Don't try to think. Just enjoy the flow of the city. Your cab will be here soon. The driver might be from a village in a nation far away. He will understand when you say you are from the country. Sometimes he too wants to beam home.

WORKOUT

STANDING NAKED in the kit-
chen, I reach both arms up to the ceiling and stretch my entire body.
I feel the pull most in my torso, my ribs lifting away from themselves,
inviting air in through my mouth and nose.

My lungs are learning to use the extra space and I can hold my
breath now for seven seconds. When I started a few weeks ago, I
could only do three. I am pleased with myself.

I move through the rest of the stretches, as amazed as I was the
first day I did them. With each motion, another rope of muscle
quickens, distinguishes itself from flesh. I count each exercise the
way a child counts treasures, concentrating for a moment on each
one, then, in the end, admiring the whole. This is the way my body is
supposed to behave, like a good companion, colluding in my
pleasure.

I move from the kitchen into the living room, step aboard the
treadmill set up there, and begin my walk into the morning. I am up
to eleven luscious minutes. Keeping my pace steady, I make a quick
survey of the room deciding which object to look at today: the piano;
the picture of Aaron; the picture of Andrew. The bookcase. The
fireplace.

Any will do, but the one I choose does not stay in my mind for long. As my legs and heart keep their own pace, my brain skitters along another path, notions and memories leaping in and out of focus the way children do on a long walk.

Today, as often, I have to fight the magnet thought of last summer. With the ease of a germ, it invades my daydreams. I was sick. I got sick in May and I didn't get well until October, and all those long months a rogue virus played about my body. In a diabolic version of hide and seek, it coursed through my bones one week, joints the next and on into corporeal systems I didn't even know I had.

There was no control. Medicines relieved symptoms. Sleep was sanctuary. There was little pain, only a slow slipping away from sentience. Often my mother came to mind. When she was my age she got sick and did not get well. From her bed, she fretted about laundry. At night, when the pain rose like a full moon and shone on everything in the house, she plied the hallway, weeping as silently as she could. I was too young to help. And now I was too sick to care about dying.

My doctor said I would not die and I believed him, yet I thought about death. The life I had been acting in continued to go on, a movie I had stepped out of, and was now watching. I had no desire to get back into it.

I did not know how sick I had been until I began to get well. After the first two months, in almost human fashion, the virus weakened. Now I understood my mother's tears. Her pain was double: the grip of cancer on her bowels, and the grip of desire squeezing at her heart. I wanted to cook dinner, but could only go as far as getting the food out. I started to town one day, just for the diversion, and less than halfway there turned around and came back. Fatigue pulled me down with the ease of gravity.

This is what the man was talking about on the radio one day. His job was to demolish buildings. He used implosion, rather than explosion. "They want to come down," he said. "It has taken all of our wits to get them to stay up. We only have to allow them to fall."

I had seen films of his work, great buildings standing firm against the sky one minute, then, hit in the gut, breath sucked in, they knelt for the briefest of moments and then crumbled into a heap of rock.

Dead. Dead buildings. Just let gravity do its work.

I pick up my pace on the treadmill, keeping an eye on the pulse monitor. A tiny black heart flashes with each heartbeat and the number on the display pops down and up and down, even though I seem to be keeping an even stride. That is how my recovery went, one day better, the next day worse, but in the long pull, my energy began to hold.

Concurrently, my patience failed. When I tried to pick a cleaning brush from its cup and it pulled three others with it and they all fell into the sink like jack straws, I got a hammer and nails and pounded a peg for each one right into the side of a cupboard.

I slept well that afternoon, the way I did after I threw away my mother's waffle iron. It had been sitting on the cupboard for two weeks, the burned scraps of the last waffle disaster refusing to dissipate into air, even though I was so utterly ill. I started to clean it one day, but it was just too hard. "She has been dead for thirty years," I thought out loud, and plunged the beast into the trash.

It was after that that I began to work again, although it would be a long time before I got any work done. First I had to just sit at my desk. It was like coming home after a long stay far away. Then I always walk into each room, a little afraid of its emptiness, and hope that there is enough in my heart to fill the space.

Gradually, I began to feel desire. I wrote letters, just to hear the keyboard click. I wrote a very bad poem about being sick, and then another one, not so bad. And then one day I went to work in earnest and I lasted all day, but at the end I wrapped myself in a blanket of sadness: now I had to live. Debts in fact and debts of the heart would have to be paid.

The pickup reel picked up speed and I had a hard time keeping up. I had not pulled a weed all summer, or even walked to the mailbox. All of my muscles, from my legs to my heart, were slack. I got out of breath just brushing my hair.

The bell on the timer on my treadmill rings. I slow down, watching the numbers on the pulse monitor drop to one hundred and then below. Getting off the machine, I make three cool-down tours around the circle of rooms that is our house and stop finally in front of the long mirror. I unpin my hair. It unfolds itself all the way down to my waist. I pick up my brush and begin to work the sweat and oil on my scalp down through the damp strands. My body is also slick with labor.

In my chest, my heart thumps.

ONE WINTER

October 12

IT STARTED as rain. Then flakes began to mingle with the water. I would still not have said it was snowing, but when I looked out from the kitchen window across the field and then across the farther field, the road there was concealed in a white mist.

Snow. Now, a few hours later, it surrounds me with its thick falling. Even the close field fades. Only tree limbs and twigs, embroidered in white against the white weave of the sky, stand out.

But October is too early for a keeping snow. By afternoon, the field is again beige and brown. The lilacs have shaken off their white burden and straightened up. The skeletons of asters and goldenrod again appear to be simple, their minute distinctions, temporarily limned by the snow, lost again in the camouflage of their own color.

November 7

THE DAY is almost spent. Bill and I lean back into the hot water of our little spa and look out through the window into the dark. As always, we have turned on the outside light and snow is passing through its field.

It is a thin snow, falling not in flakes that tumble off each other but rather in segregated dots, spaced evenly in their straight line descent to earth. The first ones down melted, but enough have fallen to overcome the warmth still leeching out of the soil. Some parts of the yard are already covered. By morning, the rest will be graced.

November 8

I GET UP eager to survey the first full swaddling of the land, but during the night, when no one was watching, the snow quit falling. The heat that never stops rising out of the ground won out, and the brown grass is exposed again to light.

In spite of that, the lake did freeze over while we slept. I sit at the kitchen table and let my eyes leap the yard, the hill, and the swamp that separate us from our bay of Mud Lake. At first I think it is still open. Something is moving there. It could be water picking up the breeze. But when I stare long enough at one spot, I see it is the remnants of last night's snow skating across a rigid patch of blue.

I turn to the cookbook shelf and search for the thin, grey spine of the house journal I started keeping the year we moved here. On the inside front cover I add another line to the column marked "Bay Frozen," and enter today's date.

I am pleased to have this day acknowledged. It is Andrew's birthday, his twenty-seventh. I let myself remember. We drove in to the hospital late in the evening. Snow was falling, great thick clouds of it roiling around our Volkswagen and illuminated in waves as we passed under the street lights of the city of Minneapolis. Early the next morning, Andrew was there, and by this time of morning, seven o'clock, where I am now lingering over tea, I was curled on my side in bed, with Andrew in the crook of my arm, his mouth working at my nipple.

Thanksgiving

ONE YEAR, at Thanksgiving, we had three feet of snow on the ground. On Thanksgiving Day, the temperature lifted as though on purpose and the snow crystals softened. Snow man weather. Michael and Vivienne and Kathy and Scott and Chabin and Hazel and Bill and I put on our boots and parkas and mittens and scarves and while the turkey skin finished crisping, we went out into the yard and went to work remaking the leavings of nature's storm into our own image.

Those snow folks held all winter long, although Vivienne's duck eventually disappeared under the wrappings of a new blizzard, and the charcoal briquette eyes of the snow man and snow woman pulled in the warmth of the sun and fell out.

This year on Thanksgiving Day we have no snow, either wet or dry. I have learned though, that the swamp grasses, left uncovered, continue to change color. The saffron that followed the autumn green has given way to amber. And this year, instead of playing in the snow before dinner, we go out to walk after the fact.

There is no moon, but stars stud the sky. As we ease our way down the driveway, our eyes get used to the dark. We are free then to look up, and in our human way we look for landmarks in the heavens.

The Big Dipper is stretched horizontally along the northern horizon. We count upward five times the length of the two stars that make up the right hand side of the bowl, and find the north star. It is innocuous, not very bright, and dimmed even more by the litter of other lights around it.

At the end of the driveway, we turn south onto the road. Betty and Barry turn back. They will loll in the house with Bill, who stayed there. Helen and Chery stride out. CarolAnn and Michael and Josef and I dawdle.

The wind is not kind. It comes at us down the road, as though driven. Except for Josef, we do not mind. From inside his blankets he sets up his own cry. Maybe if he were more than four months old he would find solace in Orion striding the arc of heaven above us. Michael talks to him. CarolAnn and I walk close together, silenced by the splash of a single star in its final race across the sky.

Back in the living room, our cheeks keep their cool. Josef sighs in CarolAnn's arms and drinks himself to sleep. Chery and Helen too find their way home. We still have pie to eat. Pumpkin the color of a snowless meadow in mid November. Whipped cream, slick on the tongue as kisses in the night. Hot, black coffee.

Winter Solstice

TOMORROW IS solstice, the official beginning of winter. In Minnesota, we usually consider that a joke. By December 21 the lakes have been frozen for nearly two months, and it has been good skiing for at least four weeks. Rather, for us, solstice cuts the winter in half. Even though the hump, January, is still ahead, days from then on do get longer. Yesterday, though, it snowed all day, and then all night, the first keeping snow of the winter, and for once the prophecy of the calendar is fulfilled.

Today, the curtain of clouds overhead is again reinforced by falling snow. Although there is no wind, there is enough energy in the fall itself to mask the treeline that is our usual horizon. This morning we are delimited by the duck house to the west, the old garage to the north, the maple grove to the east, and the bone yard of felled elms in the field to the south.

The snow marks everything in between. The bluebird house holds a cap half its height. The last of the Hallowe'en pumpkin, long since melted into itself, and barely hanging onto its bench, leers under a white shawl. Each dried flower stem on the four foot tall tiger lily stalks blooms again.

All day long I watch as the earth fills up with this white gift. Following three summers of drought, a winter without water would not be a blessing. The big trees were already weakened. In August their leaves were thin, and in autumn they gave in quickly to cold and wind.

Late in the afternoon I go out. It is time for chores, the feeding of the ducks and birds, the bringing in of wood. I pull my heavy boots out of the back of the closet, shake out sunflower seeds stored in the toes by mice, slip my feet into the padded caves, wrap the extra length of the shoe string twice around the top of the cuff and pull tight.

Hat. Scarf. Lined leather gloves. The tea kettle off the wood stove. The wood cart.

There still is no wind. The snow still falls. Leaving the cart by the back door wood pile, I go stand away from the house. Lift my head and listen.

Snow eats sound. The only noise is the rub of my jacket arm against the breast of my jacket. I hold the hot tea kettle out from my side and walk down to the duck house. The path I make today will serve us all winter. Even after blizzards it will show, a sunken shadow of a scar leading from one house to the other.

With my boot I drag the snow away from the sill, pull open the door and join the ducks. Mindy glares from a perch. Moe hisses from a corner. I tell them the snow is not my fault, even though it was my idea. From the can in another corner I scoop out corn, dish out old bread. Refill the water dish.

I give the path back to the house another going over, and then make another path alongside the house to the bird feeders. Chickadees reluctantly yield to me and from the can by the rose bush, I put out more seed.

Again I stop to listen. Now, accustomed to the outside air, I can hear grosbeaks fidgeting in the trees and down the hill a woodpecker at work. I return to the back door, fill the wood cart and tug it in over the sill.

One last task. I tighten the strings around my boots, take the house broom from beside the door, and let myself out again into the white arena. This time I strike out northwest across the yard. The snow is deepest there, and because it is so light and dry it sifts down into my boots with the ease of water. There the warmth of my blood melts it and the cold of the leather freezes it and ice socks form around my ankles. I keep going, though, straight toward the satellite dish.

Snow lines the entire inside surface of the bowl, weighing it down imperceptibly, but enough so it will not catch all of the image cast down here from space. I lift the broom over my head and sweep the dish, dodging the chunks and sheets that follow gravity's command and seek earth. The dish wobbles, then settles, in alignment again with the plastic stars we humans have tossed into the heavens.

Then I return to the house, nailing down another snow path that we will use all winter, even though the snow that is still falling will fill it up tonight. By the time I am back in the house, it is dark. I turn on inside lights, and then the television. The picture is clear. There is a national weather report in progress. California is unseasonably cool. Tornadoes in the southwest. December drizzle in New York. In Minnesota it is, at last, winter.

December 23

THE SOLSTICE snow fall lasted three days. Now, except for brief flurries, it has stopped. Measuring by the depth of the path to the duck house, I would say we got about eighteen inches. The last day there was drifting. A skirt is wrapped around the base of every deciduous tree and white bunting loops around the outer reach of the lower branches of the pines. Under their branches, the ground is bare.

Shadows come easily when the sun's arc is so low in the sky. Down in the swamp, even the thin weeds are duplicated on the snow, and the creek that cuts through the middle of the swamp is betrayed by the shadows from drifts held in place by the open space of frozen water.

Snow settles in weather like this. The caps on the bird houses and tree trunks soften into curved mounds, and the snow chunks churned up by the plow lose their edges. Even the sky seems forgiving, the hard blue at zenith dwindling down at the horizon to a soft white.

January 17

"GARBAGE NIGHT." Bill has loaded the cans into the pickup. I take them down to the "curb," an expression left over from my city upbringing.

At the end of the driveway, I pull the cans out of the truck and stand them in a cluster between the driveway and the ditch. There is no wind, not even a breeze, and in the ultra cold, minus 25, I hear a branch crack in the woods a quarter mile up the road. Looking that way, north, I can see the neighbor's light blinking through the bare tree branches. To the east, way across the field, through some trees and on the other side of county 201, I can see the Christmas lights on two houses. South is black. West, behind me, our own house takes shape in the light from the living room.

I hold my breath in the silence and tilt my head back to scan the sky. It is almost blue, a dark, dark blue. A half moon hangs at zenith. Instead of the aura I expect to see, there is a stark white chalk line intersecting the paper-white disc.

Strange. I follow it out into other space. It is a circle...a circle that cuts through more than half of the northern sky and cuts through another circle, one that encircles the entire night sky, with the moon precisely at its center.

I gasp. My lungs leap at the cold air. My heart beats faster. The earth curves away from me, and I am ringed like a white half moon by one white circle, intersected by another, and the two circles intersecting.

January 25

IT IS early morning; pre-dawn. Letting myself wake up, I sit and stare out the window to the left of my desk. The sky is uniformly grey. Then a fuchsia smudge appears due southeast on the horizon. I sit up straight and peer at it. Flames dart into the treetops, and I think it is a fire, but then a clear curve of saffron light pushes the smudge upward and in moments, just moments, the sun is there, above the horizon, and the color is all gone, and the sun itself is so white that, moving up the ladder of space, it pushes even my glance away.

On the other side of the few inches of walls and windows that cloister me, the temperature is 28 degrees below zero. There is some wind, enough to pull the smoke out and away from the downstairs' chimney, and to drag it across the roof, past my second story office windows, and scatter it in the yard to the east of the house. There it dissipates in the light from the sun that has now climbed free of the tree line and will pace me through the day.

February 25

THE SNOW is sinking. Even though we get new batches of it that bring the levels back up, the lengthening daily tenure of the sun, and the intractable seasonal warming of the earth ball gradually consume winter's coverlet. The oldest snow, that closest to the ground, has shrunk away from the larger snow mass, opening long, honeycombed passages occupied by mice and moles. Topside of that invisible country, snow that is more than a few days old is crusty and slick.

Today it is twenty degrees above zero. Last night, new snow fell. Eating breakfast, I watched a redpoll at the kitchen window feeder, scuffling around in the fluff, releasing the little obsidian ovals of "black sunnies," the oily sunflower seed preferred in northern Minnesota by birds and bird watchers.

I slip on my boots over my socks, my parka over my nightgown, forsaking scarf, cap and mittens in favor of a quick round of the feeders. As I approach the one at the kitchen window, the redpoll reluctantly moves to the Russian olive and keeps watch. A chickadee joins the vigil and scolds at me: "dee, dee, dee; dee, dee dee." Before I move around to the corner of the house to the other feeders, the chickadee has snatched a seed and is back in the olive, breaking it open. The redpoll has retaken its position and is leisurely picking through the new fare, mixing the hulls it empties with the ones yet to be cracked.

The redpoll is one from a flock of one hundred or more that has been with us most of this winter. This morning, they wait impatiently for me to finish my chores. From the apricot and the olive, even from the oaks and maples farther away, I can hear their conversations.

Back in the house, I shake the cold out of my nightgown, and make a pilgrimage to each of the feeder windows. The redpolls have rushed in like wind. At the living room platform, they crowd each other, nudge and bustle, come and go. Their fist sized brown bodies soak up the sun that their iridescent ruby caps throw back to the sky. Their blush chests pump up and down with the task of their picking. Seen at a glance, they could be a flock of red hearts beating.

March 2

IT IS not winter anymore. The snow that still covers much of the yard is pocked and hollow. Kick it with your boot and the crystals shatter and fall like pennies dropped from a child's hand. The snow that had worked its way even under the skirts of the pines is gone. Every tree, every stump, even the flower pot left out in the garden marks the center of a brown bull's eye. Gaining height in the sky, the sun stores itself in every dark object, and the heat radiates out, and the snow backs off.

The birds have begun the changing of the guard. The redpoll flock is thinned, and this morning one evening grosbeak hung out with the pine grosbeaks that have been here all winter, but will not stay for the summer. The grey squirrels have given up their lassitude, and fill the trees with the making of their love.

My habits change too. I look for excuses to wander out of doors. Straighten the bird feeder that has been going atilt. Stack split wood we'd been content to leave in a heap. Call Bill to come look: where the snow has pulled away from the west wall of the house, day lily sprouts are up two inches.

Those fools, I think. It is only March. There will be more snow. There will be more cold. But they don't care. The sun is calling to them. The earth is pushing at them. Winter is a memory. Spring is their job.

I pull my sweater closer around me. The bright sky and warm afternoon lured me out without my jacket. Now the sun is near the horizon, and I am getting cold. Still I linger, happy for nature's reliable resurrection, sad at the passing of the quiet faith of snow.

HIPPIE REDUX

HE TRIES to say it as nicely as he can. We are talking about my business. I say that someone who dresses more conventionally than I do could probably make twice as much money. His eyes move from my un-made up face and loosely knotted hair down past my nubbly sweater, that is supposed to conceal my bralessness, to my slacks and finally my socks and walking shoes.

"Yes," he says. "A retread hippie can't really expect to make it in sales."

A retread hippie. We sign the final papers — he is buying my office supplies business. Silently, I hope he drowns in red ink and yuppie water, but I know we are both right. I could have made more money wearing hair spray, a bra, pantyhose and heels.

Outside in the sunshine, I hoist myself up into the pickup and head for home, but the epithet sticks in my head. Retread hippie. So that's what a woman is called who dresses for comfort and safety. For four winters I drove around the northern third of Minnesota selling office machines and supplies. What kind of a fool would wear a skirt at twenty-five degrees below zero, driving on a road with no town for twenty miles? Not this fool.

Of course, it is more than weather that keeps me out of skirts. When it is warm outside, I don't wear them because I do not shave my legs. This is a personal issue with me, not a public statement, so I keep my hirsute limbs under wraps. In fact, I work hard to keep my clothes from being an issue. A few years ago, for my son's formal wedding, I even searched out an appropriate, dressy outfit.

I found one, a silky number with a not too flouncy skirt, and I looked good in it. The untucked top flowed down to my hips, so the proximity of my breasts to my waistline was not too obvious. The clerk and I were pleased. We stood and looked at my reflection in the long mirror. Our gazes screeched to a stop just below the hemline where the unruly tangle of my leg hair stood out in the static electricity of the dry store air.

I couldn't wear tights. The wedding was in the summer, in California. "Do you have textured panty hose?" I asked. They did. I read the chart on the back and calculated my height and weight. "Do you have queen size textured panty hose?" They did not.

For the next two weeks, I rued many times my twenty pound violation of my Weight Watchers' goal. There seems to be a law: women who are not slender shall not wear textured panty hose. I settled for a "large." The crotch rode dangerously close to my knees, and the waist band hugged my hips, but at the wedding I didn't walk funnier than the other women. The ceremony was outside. I wore flats. They wore heels, and maintained their balance in the grass by walking tiptoe, their arches straining to gain an extra half inch above ground zero.

For a few moments in that shopping week, I considered doing something I hadn't done for fifteen years: shaving my legs. I remember when I stopped. I was a single parent of two young children, going to school, teaching and learning to be a writer, and I just got tired of lathering up. The next day my legs looked like plucked chicken skin, and I had to do it again. I had better things to waste my time on. I still do, so the hair stays.

The bra I did give up during a consciousness-raising frenzy, and discovered that it feels good to be without one. I remember the pain when I took it off at night, and the weight of the tissue grabbed for support from the pampered muscles. Wearing a bra doesn't keep breasts firm, it only keeps them harnessed. My breasts may not hang high, but they do have muscle and tone.

At home I change into shorts and look for my husband in the garden. We live in the country, on forty acres of swamp, field and forest. There is a very slight breeze. I can feel it in the hair on my legs. It is one of the little contacts with nature that I cherish. I wonder how I used to feel anything, with my hair lacquered and my face caked with clay-based products. I wonder that I could think at all with the lower half of my body shrink-wrapped in plastic, depriving me of the goodly supply of oxygen that we take in through our skin.

Maybe I am a hippie. I don't even shave my arm pits, and I don't miss those little knicks and scratches that scream with recognition when infused with deodorant. But I don't flaunt it. I don't wear tank tops, or sleeveless shirts.

I pay attention to all of my wardrobe. I wear ribbed knits, patterned blouses, and camisoles, so my nipples don't stick out too much. Some women, especially blondes, can get away with not shaving their legs, but I have the hair count and color of a female gorilla, so I keep those gams covered.

Sometimes I think I have made a lot of extra work for myself, but it is no more trouble than trying to keep a drawerful of un-run nylons. Being a non-comformist, I tell myself, doesn't mean freedom from decisions and responsibility. It just means being identified by a different name. Some women are fashionable, some are contemporary. Some are casual. Some are retread hippies.

My husband stops the roto tiller and we sit in the grass and talk about the sky and the bald eagle he saw earlier. And we listen to the little birds scuffling about in the brush. I ask him if I am a retread hippie.

He lifts a hank of my hair away from my face and tucks in the kleenex that is hanging out of my shirt pocket. Don't worry, he says, now you can write full time, and writers are supposed to be a little different. Besides, you're getting older. Pretty soon you won't be odd, or even a retread. You'll just be eccentric.

Yea, I thought. Eccentric. I like that. Besides, I've noticed that old people don't have hair on their legs, not even the men. Maybe it wears off. All I have to do is wait.

CAKE WALK

I CALL it wedding cake. My friend Debbie calls it birthday cake. Some people call it bakery cake, and that's what it is...white bakery cake with white frosting. I know it has no egg yolks, and I know the frosting is made with lard...that's why it is so utterly white. But I don't know what the addictive ingredient is. Maybe it's some subtle combination of sugar and fat.

I do know that I am addicted to it. They say that alcoholics remember their first drink and I remember my first white bakery cake. It wasn't exactly mine. Well, it wasn't supposed to be. It was in the dining room...a room reserved for very special occasions. There was some grown-up event in preparation. I was little. I could barely reach onto the table. There was a silver tray full of little white cakes. Petit fours, I know now. They were so incredibly pretty: pure white, each one a little handful, and decorated with the sweetest little flowers and leaves.

Only an addict would have defied the order: don't touch. I did touch. And I ate, too. More than one. I don't remember the ultimate consequence, but I do remember my mother's skirt appearing at my side.

The next cake I remember was at a birthday party. This time it was a two-layer cake. But it had the magic combination: white cake, white frosting, and it came from a bakery. At the mother's instruction, a dime had been stirred into the batter. Whoever got it in her piece would get a prize. I didn't care about the dime or the prize. I just wanted more cake.

Of course, it is not unusual for children to abandon restraint in the face of a favorite food. I did not begin to recognize the trouble I was in until my older sister got married, and I had my first piece of wedding cake. I was a teenager at the time. I knew about restraint.

It was that first bite that did it. With it still in my mouth, I found myself sidling back toward the cake table. I had a second piece, and then a third. Only the attendant there noticed, and he seemed to enjoy my passion. He did put an end to it, though, when I started eyeing the top most piece of cake, the one with the little bride and groom on it. The one my sister was supposed to have.

She got it. But only because that waiter was so stubborn. Anyway, I was getting full. And I was beginning to experience another craving, this time for milk. As my habit refined itself, cold, cold milk became a necessary complement to a good white cake binge.

Binge is the right word for my cake eating behavior. I could go months, even years, without bakery cake. But as soon as it was in my presence.... And I have never learned restraint. I have, in fact, embarrassed myself. Some years ago I was at a reception. I had wondered a few days before if there might not be some white bakery cake with white frosting. If so, it would probably be a sheet cake...long, wide, single layer, with plenty of extra frosting available in the borders, flowers and letters. My mouth began to moisten. Maybe I would go early.

The reception was important, and fun: a gathering of old friends, some I hadn't seen for years. At first the cake was nowhere in sight. Then they brought it out, and a little ceremony was held over it...not for the cake, but for the friends gathered. I was in an adjoining room. "The cake is out," I said hopefully to the group I was with. No one cared. They wanted to know about my kids.

People started going by us with little white paper plates with white cake on it. White frosting. Flowers. I excused myself, came back with a plate and nibbled while we talked. "I think there's plenty of cake," I suggested. No one cared. I had to go back alone for seconds. Very shortly I was ready for my third helping. I had pretty much lost the drift of the group's conversation, so this time I just hung around the cake table. Really should talk to some other people too, I told myself.

I don't think anyone actually noted my cake-driven behavior. But I did. I knew that I had chosen my addiction over the solid food of good conversation. The next step was inevitable: public humiliation.

It was a number of years later. We were at a dinner party, with friends. Just a small group, eight of us at one table. Debbie, the hostess, also liked white bakery cake with white frosting. And she taught me a dangerous lesson: there is no rule against having it for an ordinary dinner gathering. It didn't have to be a wedding or a birthday or an anniversary.

We had it that night, in fact, and I had two generous pieces. So far so good. The cake sat in the middle of the table. I could have just cut another piece. But the conversation was good, too, and I was so comfortable, so at home. I didn't even know what I had done until I felt my husband nudging against me. I looked at him. He had a look of disbelief and not a little horror on his face. I became aware of my arm, my hand, my fork. They were laid out across the table. I had been dipping into the cake itself, nonchalantly breaking off one forkful at a time and eating and talking. One side of the cake was all broken down.

Debbie understood. Now we occasionally have a cake-lunch, where we just sit at the table with forks and the cake between us and a gallon of milk alongside. It is sort of like having your cake and eating it too.

Those planned indulgences may be the reason I have developed a bit of control over my cake craving. I shop at a grocery now that has a bakery right there. They always have whole cakes ready to buy. That's too much for my husband and me, and I do resist. But they also have four-packs of cupcakes with frosting that doubles the height. Perfect for dinner for two. I've bought them many times. Someday maybe they'll make it home to the dinner table.

FIRED UP

I AM sitting on the couch doing needlework and watching television. I become aware that I have stopped stitching, that I feel restless. I know what it means. I know what is coming.

I close my eyes, lift my head a little, take in a deep breath, a welcoming breath, then expel it forcefully, audibly, my lips puckered as though to kiss.

Keeping my eyes closed, I tell myself to relax. Let it come; let it pass. Heat begins to emanate from somewhere inside myself that I cannot locate. It radiates out to the surface, to every surface of my skin. I want to fidget, to get up and move, but I make myself stay where I am, stay still.

I keep my eyes closed. The heat concentrates in my face, and my chest. I try to float back: remember Lydia, I say to myself. Float back with Lydia. I take in and expel another deep breath. Water outs. My entire back is awash. Pools form under my breasts, under my knees, in the elbow hollows. My crotch is wet. Rivulets journey down my face. I open my eyes, reach for my little fan, and for a few moments bask in the blessing of moving air, but the work is too hard. My heartbeat has risen with the storm, and the effort of fanning is too much. I drop my head back; close my eyes again. Breathe in. Blow out. All the way out. Cleansing breath. Down to my toes. The sweating abates. The heat wanes. My heart rate falls off.

It is over. I keep my eyes closed, let my breath soften and slow down. I feel clean, sleepy, whole, aware of all of my body. Can feel the water cooling on my skin.

I sit up. Stretch. Wipe my face with the towel I keep handy. Pick up my needlework. Watch TV.

LYDIA CLOSES her eyes and blows out a long, deep breath. It is a signal: a contraction is starting. She sinks back into the rocker. I stand behind her, place my hands on her shoulders, and begin the litany: "Completely relaxed now, all the tension falling away. Float up on the water. Float up to my hands. Let the pain fall away, away down to the bottom of the water."

"Feel my fingers, follow my fingers." I press down with them one at a time, left and right hand synchronized: little fingers, ring fingers, middle fingers, index fingers, thumbs; repeat. "Stay with my hands, stay with me on top of the water. Float like seaweed on the water. Feel the sun on your face. Smell the water. Let the pain fall away, fall far away to the bottom of the water."

When we practiced, Lydia described to me the image she uses. Her legs get long and heavy and stretch way to the bottom of the water, like a mermaid's tail. In labor, her legs became numb.

When we practiced, Lydia told me she once had a caudal block, a spinal anesthetic, after a miscarriage.

"Completely relaxed now, Lydia. Your shoulders relaxed, your back relaxed. Find your spine now. Follow down your spine to the site of the injection. Your body remembers. Remember the numbness spreading like sunlight down your spine, into your pelvis, into your groin. The pain falling away. Your body remembers this."

"When we get to the spot on my spine," said Lydia, "I tie a ribbon around it and pull tight, and the anesthetic spreads down and around."

She blows out another long breath, a cleansing breath. Mine overlaps hers, my hands stroking her hair, rubbing down her arms. She rests. I rest. Then she pulls in a fresh long breath, the welcoming breath, and blows out. "Completely relaxed now Lydia. Remember, you will have no more pain than you are willing to bear. Let the bag of muscles do its work. Let the pain fall away. Come up to my hands. Float on the water. Feel the sunlight. Smell the water."

"Smell the water." Our nostrils already sweet with the smell of birth. Ben loves that smell. When I go home that night, it is on my clothes. I hold my shirt to my face and inhale. Baby. This is the smell of a new baby, the smell of birth, of birthing.

Between contractions, Ben leans down to Lydia. During contractions, he watches and waits. He takes care of me. Brings me water and muffins. Talks Lydia through contractions when I go for a walk.

But it isn't the same, he says. Lydia welcomes me back. Her shoulders settle under my hands. She lets the pain fall away. Face relaxed. Eyes, brows, lips. Mouth open, letting in the sunlight, opening like a flower, showing the cervix, the birth canal how to open; throat full of sunlight. Floating on the water, head dipped back, the water lapping against her brow.

At first the nurses think she is not in labor. She looks like she is sleeping. Later, not much later, they prepare the room. "This might go pretty fast." They watch us, admire us. Lydia is so powerful, accepting my voice over her pain. I drink her trust and give it back.

We move to the bed. "Let your arms float out on the water," and I draw my hands down her arms. "Feel the sun on your face, feel the sun on your chest," and I press my hand on her breast bone and later she will tell me it felt like sunshine.

Later she will tell me, "You got closer, and closer. At the end, your lips were on my ear."

I put my lips to her ear. "Come with me Lydia, float on the water."

She holds on to Ben all through the pushing. Presses against his arms as though to open a door. Between pushes, my hand like sunlight on her chest. "Push now, push now," blood rising to her face like fire. The pelvic gate heaves open. Joseph born.

Lydia taking my face into her hands, pulling me close. Her eyes an ocean in which I swim.

"HORMONE STORM," I explain. As president of the board, I am at the head of the table, managing the agenda. I do not break stride as I wipe the water from my face. But they are interrupted: "Are you all right?"

"It's just hormone storms. I'm not having a heart attack. It will go away. And it will come back." I blow out a short breath and resume the discussion. Reluctantly, they follow me. Are relieved, I think, when my face fades from ruby to pink. Don't notice when I pull my vest back on, in the frigid wave that follows the heat.

BOTH MY older and younger sisters had hot flashes before I did. Larry told how Gretchen would throw off all the bedclothes and turn the ceiling fan onto high. He'd be hanging onto the bed so as not to be blown off. And then Gretchen would be covered, curled into a sweet sleep, oblivious to the hurricane.

Gretchen and Karen and I stayed at a hotel together, out celebrating Gretchen's fiftieth birthday. Gretchen and I shared a bed. Neither of us wanted to sleep with Karen, but in the middle of the night we were wakened anyway. Covers thrashing. Then "click-click-click-click." At first we thought it was the ventilation system. It was Karen's fan. Then a scurry and the gathering of covers. Then silence. For awhile.

Nesting, my husband calls it. I get on my belly, poke at the pillows I keep at each side of my head, on call for later. Grapple with the sheet and the blanket and quilt until I'm covered up to my ears. A sigh. Silence. Shoulder shrugging. One foot out from under the covers, followed by knee, by thigh. Whole leg swung out and on top of the covers. Arm swung out, throwing covers back. Legs pushing covers off. Naked in the night air. Floating on a skin of water. "Float with Lydia. Float with Lydia on the water." Drifting into sleep. Aroused by air gone cold. Reach around for covers. Arrange around shoulders. Fall into wet, warm sleep. For awhile.

IT IS a labor of sorts. A slow motion, low key labor. Mine has lasted two years so far, segueing from mere sensations of being oddly warm now and then to intense heat storms. For awhile these were preceded by nausea, the same nausea of early pregnancy, and left me feeling restless and angry. Finally the sweats began, grateful release in a body cleanse. They are more visible to others, but less bothersome to me.

I have quit trying to make them stop. For a long time, going to sleep at night, I imaged them away. I wanted to finish the task. To leap over the experience. I told my ovaries to retire. To check out. I shrink wrapped them in plastic and stored them away. Cancelled the egg call. Disconnected the thermostat. The flashes themselves, I tried to ignore.

Then the sweats started, and I thought about Lydia, and realized a hot flash lasts about as long as a labor contraction. I tried a welcoming breath. I floated on the water. I gloried in the ethereal calm after the storm.

How to explain this to others? It is not like a fever. It is not like the heat of a tropical sun. Sauna. It is like a sauna. A personal sauna. A private sweat lodge. I laugh to think how hard humans work to create this state, and how women have it and have not been happy about it.

Of course, saunas and sweat lodges are used by choice, but many times during the day and at night I can let myself be carried away. The other times, at meetings, at my desk, making dinner, I make a silent acknowledgement, and go on. At night, going to sleep, I wonder what it would be like if we honored the hot flash. At a meeting, a woman would blow out an audible breath, and everyone would stop, and turn to her, and she would close her eyes, and they would envy her as she floated into the storm, and then they would welcome her back, and mop her brow, and ask her about the place she had been, and she would be sorry it was over, and would hope it would not be too long before the next one.

MENOPAUSE IS the first of the coming-to-full-circle that is human aging. As in pre-menarche, I am not fecund. I do not measure time by ovular cycles, by the blood wash of the uterus. I am innocent again. And again, I am come of age, am come into myself, a self for whom I have always been preparing.

Hot flashes have taught me patience. And how tough I have become. I will be ready for infirmity. Until then I will wallow in the years of calm earned by the weathering of this long storm. And if I get caught in a downpour of pain, I will remember Lydia. I will place my hands on my chest. They will feel like sunshine. And then I will dip my head back and float on the water.

WHEN
LIFE BEGINS

Ally Adams

IT IS April 9, 1989. My son
calls from Washington, D.C. That is not where he lives. He and his
wife live in Sacramento, California, where they go to school, and
work, and stretch forward with their twenty odd years of life each.
They struggle to see beyond themselves, and struggle to decide how
they want to be as human beings on planet earth as the stage of the
twentieth century narrows to its closing point.

Above my desk is a picture of this boy at age seven, with his four
year old brother and myself. We are wearing black arm bands. We
are sitting on the ground, wrapped in parkas and scarves and mittens. It is October or November and in northern Michigan the leaves
are gone, the grass yellowed. Behind us white crosses stick out of the
half-frozen earth, one for each man and woman from the area killed
in the Viet Nam war. Even in the isolated upper peninsula of Michigan, on that day in 1970 scores of people came to a rally that
repeated itself in larger and smaller versions all across the country.
We did not really expect it to matter, to end the war in Viet Nam, but
we did it anyway, because it mattered to us.

116

Now, almost twenty years later, Andrew and Debbie are in Washington, D.C. participating in the pro-choice rally prior to the Supreme Court action that will put Roe v. Wade back on the auction block.

Last night, before Andrew called, my husband and I watched reports of the rally on the network news. At one point the camera came to rest on a small field of white crosses, exactly like those we had used in the Viet Nam demonstration. I thought at first they were put there to represent the women who had died from illegal abortions, but they were not. They were put there by the anti-choice demonstrators, to represent the "dead babies."

The old anger rose in my throat. What about the dead women? What about the dead women? What about the woman in the picture that I cannot erase from my mind? It was taken before abortion was legalized. It is in a public bathroom. The woman is down on her knees and elbows, her face cradled in her arms, her buttocks raised toward the camera. She is naked. There is a pool of blood beneath her crotch. She is dead.

WHEN I was first married, in the early sixties, my husband's grandmother asked me if I took those new birth control pills she had heard about.

"Yes, Nana, I take them."

"I cannot imagine what it is like," she said, "to not worry about getting pregnant. I worried about getting pregnant almost all of my life." She had two daughters, then a hiatus of thirteen years, then three sons in a row. "I thought they would never stop coming," she told me.

Like the picture of the woman in the bathroom, Nana's voice will not leave me: the sound of fear does not deteriorate with time.

YEARS AGO, I had a tubal ligation, so I do not worry about getting pregnant. And if I do get pregnant, and abortion is illegal, I have enough money to get one anyway. And I am closing in on menopause. Safe on three counts.

I have not always been so secure. My memory of the days of Viet Nam moratoriums and demonstrations is riddled with flashes from another revolution: I was in my late twenties. I had two children, but I was just beginning to come to life. The women's movement was underway. In Marquette, Michigan, a town surrounded by hundreds of miles of forest wilderness, women began to talk to each other, in consciousness raising groups. Marriages dissolved, both figuratively and legally. A male friend asked me the classic question: "What do you want?"

I stared at him. His wife and I were in a group together. I had just left my husband. She would leave him in a few months.

I could not answer him. I only knew I was right to leave. I knew that it hurt my husband, and my sons, and my mother-in-law who was my friend, and I knew that it would not stop my pain. I did not have money, I did not know what I would or could do, I could not imagine being happy, and I left anyway.

I HAVE never had an abortion. When I was eighteen I had unprotected sex for three months and did not get pregnant. Then I got birth control pills. Then I got married, and had my two babies, and took pills in between, and after that I had an intra-uterine device inserted. Through twelve monthly ovulations times seven years that little twist of white plastic kept my uterus swept clean of fertilized ova. Since then, for seventeen years, the eggs have stopped short at the knot I had tied in my fallopian tubes. I wanted two children. I had two children.

I like to think that I am a smart woman, but I know that I have been luckier than I have been smart. In the beginning of my sexual life, I did not understand ovulation. My friends and I talked a little: could you only get pregnant with your period, or was it the other way around? I did not worry about it. Babies were not in the equation.

I was lucky that time on two counts: I did not conceive, and I had an older sister who insisted that I acknowledge the correlation between sex and reproduction. I got birth control pills.

At the time, I did not feel that the fates had smiled on me, nor did I when I didn't get pregnant too soon between babies, or in the gap between birth and birth control after my second son was born. It took the better part of my first half century to see how ingenuous I had been. Even my presence at the Viet Nam protests was more the outcome of passion than reason. I was not dumb, not smart. I was just of the times. We marched one night in a candlelight parade. We had been denied a permit to go through downtown. When we got to the corner where we were supposed to turn, and where we intended to turn, we were met by state highway patrol officers. A half dozen of them spanned the intersection, kneeling on one knee, rifles restless in their hands.

I was afraid. I suppose they were too. Kent State had not yet happened, but was broached at that crossing. Twenty years later, I wanted Andrew and Debbie to go to Washington, to march for women, and to march for themselves. I didn't want them to be afraid, but I wanted them to be afraid. "Pay attention," I said. "Trust your-selves. If it feels hinky, get away, get away."

I DO not know when life begins. I do know that without legal abor-tion, women die. They risk this for the same reasons all humans risk death: out of fear; for freedom; for glory; for power; for love; in anger; out of hate; out of pride; in hope.

We do it in war. We do it to protect ourselves. We do it even when it grieves us. We do it because even though we cannot explain it, we know it is the right thing to do.

We do it because the future is forever opening out in every direction around us, and because all life is potential, even that which is already quick.

I do know what I want: the right, the ability, the courage to choose.

WITNESS

OCTOBER TWELFTH. Columbus Day. Whose fine irony is this, I wonder, as I drive the fifty miles from my home to Itasca State Park. I am on my way to an Indian ceremony, the reburial of bones taken long ago from their graves, taken out of the calendar of decay and placed in the limbo of museum air.

I turn in at the park entrance and slow down, partly because the way is narrow and twisted and partly because of the way the light rains down through the arches of the branches that overhang this road. The leaves are at the end of their season; the chlorophyll has left them. The thin flesh of the leaf revealed, the sun falls easily through transluscent reds and yellows and browns. I roll down my window and float through the glow and silence of the park.

For awhile I do not think. Then I remember why I am here. Breaking my own rules, I am going to a funeral. I stopped doing this years ago, at my aunt's funeral. I was there, in the ante room, and suddenly I knew I could not go inside. Instead, when the others poured into the sanctuary, I let myself out through the heavy, high doors at the front of the church, and walked the city. I came upon a creek, and picked my way down to its bank, and squatted down and unearthed pebbles and threw them into the water and cried. I cried for my father, who had died last year. I cried for my son who died years before that, and for my mother who died long ago, and I decided I did not go to funerals any more.

I pull into the parking area by the Indian burial mounds and the gold of the sun and the glint of memory come together and I sit in the pickup and weep. Still, fourteen years after Aaron's death, I do not know when sorrow will overtake me. Nor do I understand how it can dissipate as quickly as it comes. I gasp under the weight of the tears, bow my head, close my eyes, feel the earth engulf me, moan. Then it is done. I lift my head, wipe my eyes, blow my nose, take a deep breath.

I close the window, open the door, decide to leave my bag in the car. I will just take my note pad. I stand up straight into the keen air of the woods, take another deep breath. Listen to the wind in the pines. I look at the note pad in my hand. Do I think this will save me from grief? I toss it onto the seat of the truck, shove the keys into my pocket and walk, arms free, toward the path that leads to the graves.

Although I am early, there are other people here ahead of me. They are gathered in the cul de sac at the end of the path. The path itself bends around the burial mounds that dot the woods and is contained by log fencing.

The mounds are unspectacular, humps of earth, about six feet wide, ten feet long, four feet tall, overgrown with flora, punctuated by small trees, and camouflaged as forest floor under an iridescent cloak of freshly fallen leaves. A wanderer here might not even see them.

Today one of them is open. One close to the fence, close to the cul de sac. The earth, that has been removed from one end and placed on top of and around the mound, is black and loose from the work of the forest — the traffic of earthworms, the multiplication of molds, the resurrection of leaf into soil.

Two men are on the forbidden side of the fence. They are Indians. Their skin is the color of oak leaves in autumn. Their hair is black, though some of one man's is also grey. They are wearing blue jeans and plaid shirts and dark colored nylon jackets. They squat at the mouth of the grave. They pick up earth in their hands and squeeze it, and crumble it back onto the earth. They close their eyes and look down. They open their eyes and look up. They take tobacco from their pouches and sprinkle it into the hole in the earth.

They do not watch the cul de sac fill up with people. I do. I watch the Indian woman with the stainless steel walker navigate the roots that cross the path. She goes a little ways past the grave site and turns around to face it and stands and waits, the dappled sunlight catching in the wrinkles on her face, and igniting her grey hair.

I watch the string of Indian children from Circle of the Earth school. They tumble into the chute of the path, quieting themselves as they get farther into the woods, and falling silent as they arrive at the place of prayer. Like the others spaced around the circle, they turn toward the open mound and watch the medicine men.

I am standing on the path, just before it enters the cul de sac. I still do not know why I am here, and am afraid to enter the circle. It is the way I felt so often in grade school and high school, as though everyone else knew something that I did not.

I lean back against the fence and pay attention again to the men by the grave. Other men have joined them. Some lean over the fence and shake hands. Others climb over, lean down, pick up a handful of earth, squeeze it, and sprinkle it around, a small rain of sorts. A young Indian couple leans against the tree in the center of the circle. They hold hands. Two white women come up the path with a stroller. They talk and laugh until the silence silences them.

Two television crews inch their way into the cul de sac. The reporters frown: they want to be respectful. They motion to the camera people, who set up their tripods between the open grave and the woman with the walker who still stands, bearing the sun on her shoulders.

The cul de sac is full. The trough of the pathway is full. The sun and the breeze are kind. We are neither hot nor cold. A chipmunk runs into the hole dug in the mound, then runs up top, perches and watches.

One of the men on the other side of the fence faces the witnesses. He asks that cameras not be used during the ceremony. Two young Indian men come up the path, making their way through the skein of red and white and blended faces. They carry cardboard boxes, new ones, shiny in the October sun. The boxes are light. The young men lift them over their heads. They hand them over the fence to the two men on the other side who set them on the ground by the opening in the earth. Inside the boxes we can see bits of bright red fabric.

"No cameras now, please."

One of the men begins to play his drum, beating it softly, inexorably, the way our hearts beat. Both men face west. They sing a song I do not know. A song none of the white people and some of the Indian people do not know. A song the news people will never know.

Those who do know sing. Then the two men turn to face north, and we turn and face north, leaves bending in a breeze, and then east and then south and then back to the grave site. And the sun falls like rain through the golden leaves.

And the two men on the other side light some tobacco, and men from the path side cross over the fence and smoke with them, and one young Indian man crosses over and braces his feet over the opening in the earth, and another young Indian man crosses over and reaches into the cardboard boxes and one at a time passes to the other young man red bundles of bones, and the other Indian places each bundle into the hole in the earth where mold and earthworms can do what museum air and curious stares cannot.

And while the Indians are bringing at last to earth the bones of their grandmothers and grandfathers, the camera man in front of the Indian woman with the walker turns on his camera. In the silence of the ceremony, we hear the motion of his hand. The camera woman next to him focuses, presses her switch. A tiny red light comes on. A ruby. An ember. A bead of blood ignited.

I feel so white. My skin dazzles. My ears ring with the whine of the take up reel of the tape that wants to keep from the earth forever the bones of the red people. I am afraid to move. I will make a scene. The medicine men are not paying attention. They are crumbling earth back to earth. The cameras are recording it, and now the cameras are the event. I move in place. Others also stir. The silence of anger replaces the silence of ceremony. One of the reporters cocks her head. She hears something. Steps forward to the camera man. He turns off his camera. Another woman steps up to the camera woman, touches her, shakes her head. The red pin prick of light goes out.

I realize that I am standing straight and tense. I lean back against the rail, move so I can see around the cameras. The cardboard boxes have been set aside. Young Indian men, one of them blond, are standing on and around the mound and shoveling the loose earth into the hole. When they are done, they use their hands to clean the last bits of soil from their shovels. Some of them squat down, squeeze a handful of dirt, sift it back to the ground one last time. Then they all, all of the Indian men, climb over the fence into the cul de sac and the news people pull in around them, a human noose, and the old Indian woman with the stainless steel walker waits for the path to clear so she can go home and sit down.

I lean farther back against the rail, wrap my arms around myself. The cul de sac empties past me. I tilt my head back, close my eyes. Lift them to the sun. It comes through my lids the way it sieves through fall leaves. I float back into the woods. I am sorry, I say. I am sorry for yesterday. And now I am sorry for today.

GATHERING TIME

IT IS a perfect day. The sky is bright, cerulean. A word that means "sky-blue."

In the fall, everything repeats itself. Skeins of geese retrace their spring passage in the sky. The frames of trees begin to show. The water in the lake thickens and holds still, in memory of winter.

At the kitchen table, we sit again as we did before summer and set out our day's work in the garden. The dreams of the seeds we planted in June have become reality. For weeks we have picked tomatoes and corn. We do not "put these by," but we do eat them. At noon and at night, we step down to the garden and pick enough goodies for the meal of the moment.

That is the pleasure of the harvest: plant it, grow it, gather it, eat it. Unlike the plans we have for ourselves, the chart for the garden bears out its promise in less than a season.

And today we will reap another pleasure: we will dig potatoes and pick squash. With no more effort than a little hosing down, they will keep for the winter.

We put the potato fork in the cart and head for the "downstairs" garden. It is on the plateau of an ancient hillside, carved out by the same hustling waters of the melting glacier that gave us the long swamp at the base of the hill. Nature is patient with her gardens. Eons ago the river that flowed here settled into lakes and the lakes into bogs and today the bogs ease into marshes and swamps. Since we have lived here willow trees have taken hold in the heavy dark hummocks and will gradually nail the wet turf to the ground.

Bill takes the fork and wades into the potato patch. I pull on my gloves and begin trailing squash vines. I remember the first time I tried it, bare handed. Eagerly, I rummaged through a fan of leaves and grabbed the crooked handle of the first squash I came to. Suddenly my palms were stinging, and I dropped the horny stem I held and stood dismayed in the center of the garden.

A soft fall breeze played by me; birds sang. My husband was bent over the earth like a giant heron stalking fish. And my hands stung. I was a city girl. I didn't know there were spines on squash stems. What kind of sweet nature is this, I thought as I trudged back to the house, found gloves, trudged back to the garden.

Seven summers of experience have taught me about nature's down side. But I never seem to be prepared for the delight of the great, green globes of ripe buttercup squashes. "Look! Look at this one!" I call out over and over again. I make little stock piles, then gather them into my arms and carry them over to the cart. I feel pregnant with them, as they shift and settle in my arms.

It is hard work. I sit for awhile on the edge of the cart and look out over the swamp. A great blue heron rises out of the reeds. It lifts easily into the air, its wings pushing up and down the way a child pumps a swing, not understanding why it works, but knowing that it does.

Bill stops to rest too, perching on the edge of a metal potato crate. We do not talk. The autumn sun lands lightly on our backs. Still aware of the weight of the fruit on my belly, I think about my children. Andrew lives his own life, far away. Aaron slipped away from us long ago. That summer I spent kneeling in the garden, giving life to small things.

Even today I wonder, how can a child die? I shake myself back and let myself wander again in the squash vines, for awhile carrying each one I pick all the way back to the cart, placing it carefully on top of the others, and touching each one that it touches.

Too soon we are done, but sooner than that we are tired. The cart is full of squash. Together we harness our hands to the cool metal bar and pull ourselves and our harvest up the hill to the house.

Bill gets the tractor and goes back down for the potatoes. I can hear the metal crates meet with the metal of the tractor scoop, then watch as he emerges over the crest of the hill, head half turned, watching both ahead and behind, shoulders atilt, his torso blended into the machinery.

I never get tired of watching this man on his machine. He settles into the cupped palms of the seat; his legs attach to the pedals. He rides his own hips the way a human rides a horse.

My breath has returned. Bill dismounts from the tractor, and we sit in the grass by the back door. In the lilac hedge by the upstairs garden, the bluebirds have come back to clean out their house. Their children are with them, and they take turns going in and out, carrying away the twigs they carried in, carrying away the tiny feathers they shed as they grew. In a few years, maybe less, their lives will be over. Their children's children will return here. Or not.

We stand up again, begin to clean the dirt from the spuds. In the dark of the cellar they will stave off the calendar. In the dark of the winter, we will climb down to them, pick them a second time, wash them a second time, return again to the garden of our summer.

Cheryl McDowell

Susan Hauser is a poet and essayist. Her poems have been published in literary journals, and her articles have appeared in regional and national magazines. Her first book, *MEANT TO BE READ OUT LOUD*, received a 1989 Minnesota Book Award. She holds a Master of Fine Arts degree in poetry from Bowling Green State University, Ohio, and resides in rural northern Minnesota.

2/99 6

6 2/99
7 3/09

2/99 ^{6}

6 2/99

7 3/09